Psychotherapy and Counselling
A Professional Business

For Alasdair, Anthony and Michael

PSYCHOTHERAPY AND COUNSELLING

A PROFESSIONAL BUSINESS

Cynthia Rogers MINST.GA, UKCP REG.,
BACP Senior Registered Practitioner,
BACP Accredited Supervisor

Group Analyst and Counsellor at
The Group Analytic Practice, London
and Visiting Lecturer at Goldsmiths College, London

WHURR PUBLISHERS
LONDON AND PHILADELPHIA

© 2004 Whurr Publishers Ltd
First published 2004
by Whurr Publishers Ltd
19b Compton Terrace
London N1 2UN, England and
325 Chestnut Street, Philadelphia PA 19106, USA

British Library Cataloguing in Publication Data

A catalogue record for this book
is available from the British Library.

ISBN 1 86156 373 6

Typeset by Adrian McLaughlin, a@microguides.net
Printed and bound in the UK by Athenæum Press Limited, Gateshead, Tyne & Wear

Contents

How much can we expect to earn? ■ Unconscious attitudes towards money ■ Negotiating fees ■ When the client fails to pay ■ Managing the finances

Overcoming inhibitions about marketing ■ Forming referral networks ■ Teaching, cards and websites ■ Promoting your therapy service

Conceptualizing time ■ Managing the paperwork ■ Using routine to provide structure ■ Managing ourselves ■ Procrastination is the thief of time ■ Rewarding ourselves

Working in a GP surgery ■ The voluntary sector ■ Working alongside other professionals ■ Mentoring ■ Beyond the consulting room

Teaching ■ Supervision ■ The supervision setting

Why isn't counselling and psychotherapy a force to be reckoned with? ■ Why bother with audit and research? ■ Committee work ■ Disciplinary complaints

Foreword

Moving from a set of beliefs to a discipline taught in university to a profession is a very complicated process. There are no short cuts. The sociology of professions teaches us that all the professions we take for granted, for example pharmacy, medicine, accountancy, architecture, go through similar stages. Bucher and Strauss (1961) point out that it is helpful to see a profession as a process rather than a 'thing', 'reification' being the deadly sin of process sociologists. Writing about a profession when you are part of it, identified with it in several ways and even instrumental in shaping its direction, is a challenging and emotionally demanding task. Writing about psychotherapy and counselling as emerging professions requires thinking about all the elements that go towards defining the scope of practice and how these are managed by the practitioners. I see psychotherapy and counselling at a point in their process where sets of beliefs and assumptions are being identified, made public and being questioned. Therapists are being asked to demonstrate more clearly what they do, why they do it and which clients may benefit from various approaches. This can seem tiresome, as hopefully we have all seen the powerful life changes that many of our clients experience through therapy, of whatever modality. Sometimes changes seem almost magical and inexplicable in everyday language, and in the same way as it is impossible to describe a painting in words, it feels impossible to convey exactly what has been happening to bring about these changes. Talking about 'the relationship' and 'the therapist's unconscious' and 'countertransference' can sound overly vague and mystical and most certainly 'unscientific'!

How can we preserve what we know is important in the psychotherapeutic process while subjecting this to the scrutiny of the evidence based practice agenda? Trying to get our heads around this while at the same time maintaining a practice and engaging with our clients – who are vulnerable, in distress and in need of our full attention – can be very daunting. For trainees and newly qualified practitioners, nervousness about taking on these responsibilities can prevent them from taking advantage of their skills, their long and expensive training, and perhaps returning to a previous profession, albeit with, one hopes, more understanding of self and others. I have observed that many other professionals just do not have these problems! They are quite confident about setting themselves up in practice, either solo or more often with others. Physiotherapists, podiatrists and accountants come to mind.

Many of these issues inform Cynthia Rogers' book. You feel that she is deeply involved in thinking about all these things and that her book is a way of sharing these thoughts with others. It is beautifully written in an accessible style, designed to bring out into the open those aspects of our work that are so difficult to discuss but yet cause so much anxiety. There is an unfortunate tendency in our profession to believe that we are super-beings, unaffected by illness, death, or more joyous life events like pregnancy and childbirth. Valuable as the 'blank screen' approach might be in facilitating transference, it quickly falls apart if the therapist is quite obviously just another human being! I have never quite understood, even though I am psychoanalytically trained myself as a group therapist, why it is so difficult to work with actual material and why it should be a problem for transference. We are all inextricably linked to each other and the therapeutic session is a microcosm of the structure that we call society. Interactive therapists, like Yalom, do not find this a problem. But the pressure to maintain the analytic stance can lead to very peculiar behaviour on the part of the therapist. Cynthia's experience, as a therapist, a teacher and supervisor and manager of her own practice, and now as a researcher of her profession, explores these dilemmas. This book is a very valuable and rare addition to the literature on the practice of psychotherapy and counselling. I was privileged to read it in manuscript and have learned from it. I am certain that it will speak to the experienced practitioner as well as the trainee. I offer my hearty congratulations to the author.

Diane Waller MA(RCA) Dip Group Psych DPhil FRSA
Professor of Art Psychotherapy and Programme
Co-ordinator Group and Intercultural Therapy,
Goldsmiths College, University of London.

Preface

Cynthia Rogers

What has to happen for counsellors and psychotherapists to prosper in the current professional era?

I would like to think that working as a counsellor or psychotherapist can be emotionally and financially rewarding. It sounds simple enough but the more hours a therapist works the more vulnerable the therapist is to the inherent stresses and strains. Running a practice that provides a living is complex in itself but how do we manage when life events or our own insecurities intrude? In preparing this book I have drawn on over 20 years of working as a therapist in different settings. What follows is a collection of thoughts about the challenges a full-time therapist, working over a number of years, may well face. I cannot offer advice or recommend that others do as I have done, but hope that I will stimulate thought.

There are four sections:

- Personal professional issues
- What can a therapist learn from business ideas?
- Diversifying as a professional therapist
- Professional roles

Life events can overtake us. We expect to be there for our clients but our lives are not predictable, and when the therapist is ill, pregnant or bereaved the relationship may have to be put on hold or take on a different quality. We may have to employ a locum, change the location of the practice or negotiate retirement, to meet our own needs. This involves emotional hurdles for us as well as our clients.

Clinical issues are crucial. The early chapters are concerned with the situations we hope to avoid but which happen with surprising frequency. None of us really want to deal with the aftermath of a completed suicide. There is a myth that if we do everything right nothing will go wrong. The reality is that disturbing events go with the territory, and my suggestion is that thinking about them in advance and knowing what they stir up will go some way to enabling us to continue thinking, should they ever happen.

Counsellors and psychotherapists, who want to earn a living, find themselves, rather like fish out of water, expected to run a business. The danger is that the counsellors and psychotherapists with business skills thrive, rather than those with therapeutic talent. As a profession we need to find a way of translating our insights from the inner world and extending them to the outer world. Maybe then we can earn a living without feeling ourselves split between the 'slightly sordid' business activities and the pure counselling or psychotherapy. In writing about the business side of a practice I have been able to draw on the experience of three talented colleagues who work both as therapists and in management consultancy, small business advice, and marketing, respectively. Somehow they have the capacity to make managing the money and developing the practice seem like common sense. We nudge our clients to explore parts of themselves that have not had the chance to develop because of circumstances. I hope this section will have new ideas for those therapists who already think in business-like terms, and enable others to own the business professional hidden inside the therapist.

Counsellors and psychotherapists work in a multitude of settings each making different demands, for example private practice, general practitioner surgeries, National Health Service trusts, the voluntary sector and mentoring. Therapists tend to stick with what they know. Moving from one setting to another can be intimidating and practitioners often limit their options through lack of information and experience. In full-time practice a balanced workload goes some way to easing the inherent tensions. I hope that thinking about what is needed to work in each of the different settings will make moving into new territory less daunting and enable therapists to enjoy a more varied and stimulating practice.

The growth of the profession has increased the demand for training. Sooner or later the chance arises to teach, supervise or serve on committees. It is vital that good clinicians involve themselves in this work. It may not come naturally at first but there are 'tricks of the trade' which make it easier. The key seems to be to develop a sense of a 'self' who can teach or supervise and then think about what one needs to bear in mind when fulfilling each of these roles, in order to do it comfortably.

The mirage of registration has encouraged the introduction of professional structures. Audit, complaints procedures and committee work are at the heart of these changes. By becoming familiar with how they work and influencing the way they are implemented we can ensure our profession remains questioning and radical rather than descending into bureaucracy.

Therapeutic practice has a unique quality that is influenced by the lure of the unconscious to retreat into timelessness, as described by Angela Molnos (1995). This is reflected in the relatively closed world of therapy. It seems likely that this atmosphere is sustained by the kind of person attracted to becoming a therapist and reinforced by the training and professional rituals. I am interested in how this culture influences our behaviour and whether the culture is shifting in response to external changes. Psychotherapists and counsellors sometimes struggle to find a bridge between what we need, and want, to do and what we feel we should be doing. We are involved in a relatively young profession with elements of an apprenticeship model. The decisions we make and the attitudes we adopt will determine the nature of the evolving profession and whether we are able to retain the challenging nature of a profession whose *raison d'être* is to undo defensive structures.

Where appropriate I have used the term therapy to cover both counselling and psychotherapy. For simplicity's sake, the masculine pronoun (he, him, his) is used for a client whenever I am not specifically talking about a female client. The female pronouns (she, her, hers) are, with some exceptions, used for the therapist. I have made reference to both individual and group therapy.

Acknowledgements

Ved Varma conceived the idea of this book and Colin Whurr made it possible. My colleagues at the Group Analytic Practice, particularly June Ansell and Meg Sharpe, supported me in writing it. The observations I have made are rooted in discussions with colleagues, or encounters with students and clients past and present, who motivated me to think further. The content is entirely my responsibility but colleagues have been more than generous in sharing their thoughts.

Diane Waller inspired me to ask questions about how the profession is changing and I am grateful to Dick Blackwell, Stephen Cogill and Sabina Strich for sharing their experience of the culture we operate in. Jane Bloom, Angela Douglas and Deborah Seed described handling difficult clinical situations. Barbara Gowland, Jackie Reiter and Val Rowe contributed their professional expertise. Linda Anderson and Jean Pennant, who worked in settings I was a stranger to, introduced me to the essential character of each.

Fiona Macintosh, Christopher Rance and Michael Wilkins were invaluable resources having therapeutic and business experience. It was similarly enlightening and constructive to think about teaching and supervision with Harold Behr, and Angela Molnos. Sandra Buchanan, Ted Few and Chris James, who each have a wonderful way with words, sustained my enthusiasm for the book and helped to ensure the words made it onto paper. I should perhaps have included a chapter about the trials of writing about therapy, but one has to stop somewhere.

I am grateful to Fiona Palmer Barnes and Routledge for permission to reproduce an extract from her book *Complaints and Grievances in Psychotherapy: A Handbook of Ethical Practice* (1998). Harry Venning's 'Clare in the Community' cartoons appear courtesy of *The Guardian* newspaper; cartoons by Mel Calman are reproduced by permission of S. and C. Calman; cartoons by Harold Behr are reproduced with his permission.

Section 1

Personal professional issues

Events in the therapist's life
When the therapist's life intrudes on the therapy
Illness
Pregnancy
Bereavement
Retirement and relocation
Locums

Clinical predicaments
Understanding suicidal impulses
Terminating inappropriate therapy
Clients who become terminally ill

cartoon © H. Behr

Chapter 1
Events in the therapist's life

Therapists are subject to the same life events as clients: illness, pregnancy, bereavement and retirement. Usually our personal lives are kept outside the consulting room and we can draw on our emotional responses and sensitivities to do the work. When we are in the midst of events, our feelings may be too close to those of our clients. Can we find a way of working, not working, or employing a locum that respects our needs whilst accommodating those of the clients?

When the therapist's life intrudes on the therapy

We have an unspoken agreement with our clients that we will be there for them. They expect to have our undivided attention for 50 minutes every week. This relentless aspect of the work is difficult to sustain over a lifetime of work. Of course we have long holidays and usually manage to save illness for the holidays. Personal commitments inevitably clash with work and we find ways round it, but the pressure remains and the opportunity to be spontaneous is seriously curtailed.

So what happens when the therapist's real life intrudes into the therapeutic process? If the therapist is pregnant, bereaved or unwell it can mean taking time off work, and clients sense that the therapist is in a different place. The clients' needs have to be managed but also the therapist has to develop a way of relating to clients to whom she is no longer quite a blank screen. The clients know, or imagine they know, the therapist is under stress. The therapist is functioning from a vulnerable position where the clients are more aware of her life outside the consulting room.

Fantasy and reality

When the therapist's or the client's reality intrudes into the shared fantasy created between the client and the therapist in the consulting room, the boundary between fantasy and reality becomes blurred, which can be disturbing for both of them. The aim then would be to find a place to stand where the therapist can manage the boundaries between fantasy and reality.

A child growing up has to become comfortable with his fantasy life and the reality of his life. Where the boundary is blurred, children experience considerable distress. Thus an actor on the television pulling a menacing face might terrify a child who can happily zap and kill aliens on a computer game. He loses sight to the fact that it is pretend. This same confusion can arise in our clients when their image of us is disturbed by a glimpse of reality.

Illness

Sudden illness robs a therapist of her usual calm and control. Uncertainty becomes the name of the game. The therapist cannot predict what the implications are of going off sick and does not know what will happen. When she is ill there are good days and bad days. It is not easy to judge when to stop working. There is a tendency to try to hang on. Facing up to serious illness can be very threatening. It is not surprising if the severity is minimized. It may feel like an issue of survival. All kinds of fantasies are stirred up by illness and there can be a reluctance to tell people just how worrying the ill health is. Rather like a mother who is afraid her children will be taken into care if she cannot cope, a therapist may not wish to say how concerned she is about her health, for fear that colleagues will wade in and take over before she is ready to relinquish control.

Work often sustains us through an illness. It provides a welcome distraction from our own preoccupation with the state and implications of the illness. The work and the clients also nourish us. Where a therapist is considering stopping work the loss of the clients, superimposed on the loss of physical health, may be difficult to bear. There are also fantasies about being found out and criticized by a locum who might be asked to see the clients.

Some therapists simply assume that they have to cope, come what may. The idea that someone could take over temporarily comes as a complete revelation. Needing help can be embarrassing, but accepting help is an important skill. Colleagues who are kind and thoughtful enable a therapist to do what she needs to do. A therapist who has to be dependent on colleagues for a short while will learn about dependency and why we and our clients find it so hard. Colleagues need to hold the certainty that the therapist and the client will survive the experience. Once the therapist returns it is important to celebrate that they have survived, however difficult it might have been.

Talking with colleagues about what might be put in place, if necessary, can help to contain the therapist's anxiety when there is great uncertainty about her health. It provides space to think about how to relinquish control and later how to return to clients in a caring and thoughtful way. It is hard to let go but it may be necessary. Therapists grow through having to do things differently. We are constrained by our bodies, and sometimes can do only the bare minimum for our clients. Surviving serious illness changes us. Therapists report feeling humbled, seeing each day as a bonus and discovering a new focus.

Of course it is particularly difficult where the interruption of the therapy repeats earlier childhood experiences. If the therapy has been focused on early bereavements, the therapist's illness will stir up the very same feelings. It may be very uncomfortable for the therapist to be the abandoning mother and to experience what it feels like to be the abandoning party. When parents die children are told, 'We have to carry on'. This is taken to mean not talking, or thinking, about what has happened. Clients use the same defence when the therapist returns from sick leave, behaving as if the therapist's absence was hardly noticed and denying the importance of what happened. The real feelings may only be worked with when some other minor abandonment happens, months later. Confusion arises over who has abandoned whom. Clients who as children went off comforting themselves in private and did not talk will do the same with the therapist, abandoning the therapist they feel abandoned them.

A therapist's vulnerability is heightened during illness. Internal and external tensions occur in thinking about fulfilling the duty of care for clients and whether the therapist is up to the task. The therapist may have to face difficulties in her internal world that overlap and mirror that of the client's. Where a potentially life-threatening illness is involved, the therapist is more vulnerable than she might otherwise be to unconscious attacks on her, or threats to her client's lives and inner worlds.

A therapist will be working close to the brink, in good faith, managing therapeutic boundaries, whilst balancing caring for her clients and herself. Not everything will go smoothly. Where there are failures in the care around the time of the therapist's illness these need to be thought about. This is not to reproach, but to explore the situation that has arisen, to look at the defences used against anxiety and the clinical consequences. This might only be possible some time after the event, when the therapist's health is more certain.

Planned surgery

Where a therapist undergoes surgery she has to manage a planned abandonment of her clients. The point at which the therapist hears the diagnosis is probably the most stressful and clients are likely to pick up unconsciously on the preoccupation of the therapist. They may express unusual concern about the therapist or suddenly become more aware of changes in her attire. The therapist may feel criticized for needing to take time out and quickly has to come to terms with being just 'good enough' and not the 'ever present' mother. If a therapist can allow herself to be held by supervision she can explore what illness means. It may be confused with weakness or shame. Where surgery is intended there may be painful feelings of failure and loss. Supervision is one space where a therapist can be given permission to grieve. The therapist can also start to recognize her limitations, and get a feel for how to balance the client's needs in relation to the therapist's absence with the therapist's need to protect herself, in order to cope with the ordeal ahead. In taking care of herself the therapist takes care of the clients.

What one tells the clients varies, but colleagues seem to have said something along the following lines: that they will go into hospital for surgery; that they anticipate being away for approximately x months before returning and that a named colleague will take their place and help the clients to continue working as they have been. The locum therapist then becomes a transitional object that can be attacked or held tightly to, but also one that keeps the relationship with the therapist alive.

Where the therapist is conducting a therapy group the group members might be able to meet for a few weeks without the therapist, but generally a locum becomes necessary. Agazarian and Peters outline tasks that are important for the replacement therapist (1981).

- To work within group 'norms'.
- To help the group work through their reactions to the absence.
- To get insight into the issues that absences raise for individuals and the group.
- To facilitate expression of grief, rage and its concomitant guilt.

Employing a locum can feel rather like negotiating with a childminder. The therapist is entrusting the locum with a precious group and would like to tell the locum how to look after each client. Ultimately the therapist has to trust the group and locum to manage between them. Doubtless the group will not resist the temptation to act out from time to time.

Clients may be shocked initially. Anger, avoidance and regression will probably follow. Genuine concern for the therapist is difficult to express because it steps outside the client–therapist role but it has a place. Personal histories will influence the particular response of each client. The therapist may not want to have any communication with her clients while she is away. However, once convalescing, some therapists find it helps them bear the guilt of the separation if a message can be sent, via the locum, which conveys to the clients that the therapist is recovering and will be returning.

Returning means taking the clients back from the locum; they will have changed and had new experiences while the therapist was away. Not everyone will be obviously delighted to have the therapist back. The locum may need support in withdrawing and being allowed to feel she can take pleasure in the task she has completed. Clients are essentially preoccupied with themselves and their difficulties, and the transference is quickly re-established. What is difficult is that the clients may be feeling many of the same feelings as the therapist, who is still angry about, and mourning the losses involved in, the surgery. The significant work is at an unconscious level. If the therapist takes the time she needs, to pay quality attention to her feelings, in anticipation of re-entering the therapeutic space, this will be unconsciously communicated to the clients who may allow themselves the same leeway.

A theoretical understanding of the meaning of each step in this difficult process is helpful. Reviewing attachment theory and the kind of attachment each client has to the therapist will give an indication of what might be expected. If the therapist can resist the temptation to succumb to overwhelming feelings of guilt, for abandoning the client, she may be able to work with the client to identify which childhood experiences the dislocation of the therapy has re-evoked, and creative mutative experiences become possible.

Pregnancy

Pregnancy is a very personal and individual event, which cannot easily be hidden from our clients. The first pregnancy is new ground for both the therapist and the clients. In the mid-1990s I and other therapists described our experience in a series of papers. In this chapter I hope to give some indication of what was learnt. (A fuller description can be found in Rogers (1994).)

Some clients pick up clues about the pregnancy early on and others demonstrate an amazing capacity for denial. For a therapist who normally discloses little of herself, telling the clients is a curious experience. Deben-Mager (1993) gives a useful review of the literature dealing with announcing pregnancy to clients. The consensus is to wait for the client to become aware but also to set some realistic limit beyond which a client's denial has to be confronted. Introducing the reality may be experienced as a psychic impingement and the denial and distress can take many forms. Dreams such as deformed women exposing themselves may emerge. Clients who are determined to forget will find themselves also forgetting sessions and fees. Etchegoyen (1993) describes how the unconscious need to protect the unborn baby from attack can get in the way of grasping the material that clients bring. Coming to terms with vulnerability and limitations, as well as mourning giving up work, enables the analysis to proceed.

Miscarriage

Some clients intuitively know about the pregnancy at a very early stage, perhaps before the therapist is ready to share the information. Miscarriage is always a possibility and can become a theme of the therapy. Will the therapy miscarry? Will the client's envious destructive attacks cause the therapist to miscarry? Clients who have had miscarriages and terminations find it particularly emotive, especially if they now have to come to terms with perhaps not having children.

Envy

Envy is part of the response and it is useful to tease out what is most disturbing for each client. Murderous impulses towards the baby are often expressed in dreams and are difficult to articulate and contain. The fear of damaging the baby is quite concrete and there can be some magical thinking that if this fear is talked about it will come true. Clients can be ashamed and embarrassed by their impulse to spoil and attack. Interestingly when the envy is carefully explored it is partly about the therapist who is getting on with her life. Transforming this envy into desire becomes an important mutative process in the therapy.

The pregnancy blurs the boundary between fantasy and reality and clients can resist interpretations, preferring to retreat into a fantasy of self-sufficiency, rendering the therapist redundant. The aggression can be split off, resulting in passive aggression, and may only emerge long after the baby is born. The clients have to deal with the fear that the therapist in her vulnerable state will not be able to tolerate their primitive feelings and that she will respond by either denying them ingress or by becoming prey to the anxiety that results from introjection of their feelings. Winnicott in his 1947 paper 'Hate in the countertransference' (Winnicott, 1975) encourages therapists to be in touch with their hatred of the boundarylessness of their clients to be able to deal with these primitive processes.

The client's individual response usually reflects the family dynamics. The client whose mother neglected her when her brother was born might ostentatiously make no demands on the therapist, while another will hide the anger behind solicitous attention to the therapist's comfort. Clients with early bereavement experiences will find the separation particularly difficult and may have trouble in believing the therapist will return. To avoid the unbearable tension and feared loss they may try to terminate the therapy or drop out. Linda Anderson (1994) describes her experience of a client who committed suicide while she was on maternity leave.

The client's preoccupation with the therapist's pregnancy can be defensive and used to avoid other issues. The therapist is in a weak position to assess this. A client unexpectedly falling pregnant at this time can be quite disturbing, especially if she is heavily identified with the therapist. Mariotti (1993) suggests that such clients are caught in a simultaneous experience of abandonment and also bodily sameness with the analyst.

Body consciousness

Work around pregnancy requires attention to the body. As clients observe the bodily changes in the therapist, their own anxieties about earlier pubescent bodies protruding in all directions are activated and can be worked with. Clients defending against these feelings may somatize. Women may identify with the therapist but men have to work hard to avoid slipping into the pushed out, neglected child position. The therapist has a real sexual partner, and oedipal work can be done that enables men to move from competing for the therapist to looking for sexual satisfaction in their own lives.

Some therapists describe the difficulty of remaining engaged with their clients as they become more maternally preoccupied. My experience was that clients' behaviour was more akin to that of the first child, who when the second is expected experiences needs and urges that have to be worked with, and who demands the reassurance of an even closer relationship with the mother/analyst. Colleagues provided the 'grandparent' support, particularly when the clients reverted to earlier dependency modes and tried to deny the progress made. I was reminded of the older child who, when a new baby is expected, reverts to playing games based on 'But I'm only a baby'.

Arrangements for maternity leave

I took three months away from my practice; other colleagues took considerably less and some managed to have the baby in the analytic break. What seems important is for the therapist to do what she is comfortable with and for there to be some flexibility. Anticipating the pregnancy, I took on more short-term work and tried to avoid taking on new clients who might have significant dependency needs. I used a locum to conduct a group and this raised issues that are discussed later in the part dealing with locums. I passed another group on to a colleague and we had to work with the clients' feeling that they were being put up for adoption when the 'wanted' child arrived. A second pregnancy is probably easier to manage because the therapist and possibly the clients have been there before. They know what to expect and have some sense that they will survive the experience.

Returning to work

Timing the return to work is difficult for a therapist who has a baby. Too soon and one fulfils the client's expectations of an over-anxious mother. Too late and there are real anxieties about whether the therapy will survive. One has to deal with omnipotent fantasies about stealing the mother/therapist away from their rival, the real baby. There is also identification with the baby. If the mother does not take good enough care of herself and the baby, the client may question her ability to take care of her clients.

Clear but negotiable expectations about when the therapist will return are helpful, especially if they fit a natural rhythm. The therapist needs to have the freedom to delay returning by a few weeks if necessary, especially when this might enable her to be there for the clients in a way that she might not otherwise be. One of the painful aspects of this relationship is the re-establishing of the analytic boundary. Having sat with the bump for months, clients are deprived of the baby who has kicked its way through the sessions.

Bereavement

Where the therapist is bereaved during the analytic break it may be possible to protect the work. Mortality will probably come into the unconscious communication but, provided the therapist can tolerate it, the clients remain consciously unaware of it and the material can be worked with safely in the realm of fantasy. It is more complex when the therapist has to take time away from the consulting room and clients become aware of an aspect of the therapist's life. What one says in these circumstances is a matter for the individual therapist. Clients know that we will not take time off lightly. Giving no information is one option. It leaves the analytic space wide open and probably tells us most about the client. However, it does mean they can imagine anything and I find the need to be slightly more containing. Finding the right language can help to hold the relationship. Phrases such as 'personal reasons', 'family bereavement' and 'due to unforeseen circumstances' set a tone that conveys: 'Thank you for your concern; this is a private matter, which I am dealing with'. A client's history and their relationship to the therapy are likely to influence what can be said. Where one is dealing with a group, each member will have their own individual concerns and reactions but they will also have one another while the therapist is away.

Whatever the therapist says, the client reacts to what resonates for them. The client who was neglected after her brother died will stop making any demands. The client who never felt his mother was there for him, and felt she was always preoccupied with herself, will be beside himself with rage. Consciously the clients will convince themselves that they are protecting the therapist and managing things themselves. However, this covers massive aggression. This can be tricky to work with because the aggression is expressed in a way that is designed to frustrate the therapist and prevent her working with the material.

It is particularly complicated where the client who needed to know all the family secrets finds out why the therapist was absent. It is difficult, at the best of times, to know what to say to someone who is recently bereaved. What on earth does a client say to a bereaved therapist, who is also experienced as abandoning? The client is likely to be torn between relating to the bereaved therapist and to the transference figure. The 'as if' element can go out of the window and assumptions are made about the bereaved therapist which are entirely projections, but not recognized as such.

A therapist's unexpected absence produces a wealth of transference material, which needs working with. Where the reality intrudes it becomes very complicated and the bereavement becomes re-enacted in the therapy or the group. The fear of the wish to damage the therapist may cause clients to withdraw from the therapist. Much of this can be worked through later when there is a break or another session is cancelled. It needs to be safe for the clients to talk with real feeling about what the absence has stirred up.

Illness in the therapist's family

Having a relative who is seriously ill or dying is almost more difficult for a therapist to manage than the ensuing bereavement. The therapist has to miss sessions unexpectedly and judge where her priorities lie. I think it is important to take as much time as is needed. At a time when I knew someone close to me was dying, I conducted the most extraordinary group. They talked about how you talk with someone who is dying. A group member had a friend with a terminal diagnosis, and I just sat and listened. I had been in two minds about whether to continue working that week. Listening I realized that I was introducing a level of unconscious communication such that it would not be prudent to continue. It was a wonderfully therapeutic session for me. I took their supervision and their unconscious advice, cancelled my sessions and went home. I arranged a locum for another group I was due to conduct. He conveyed a message and held the group until I could return.

Retirement and relocation

Therapists enjoy their work, and retirement is often approached with some sadness and reluctance. It generally seems to follow a pattern of staged withdrawal. Training analysts have some responsibility to see a training client through their entire training, so not taking on this work is often a first step. Something similar occurs with very difficult and disturbed clients. This might allow therapists to cut down to three or four days a week or reduce the anti-social hours they work. Having amassed considerable experience they will be in demand as supervisors and to serve on committees etc. The time to write is often valued. Drawing up a five-year plan to work towards retirement can help with saying 'no' to interesting pieces of work. Does the new piece of work move the practice towards or away from the direction it needs to take? A living will, which describes what should happen in the event of the therapist not being able to see clients, is reassuring to colleagues who are supporting the process of retirement.

Taking on clients from a colleague who is retiring

The primary aim is not to cause too much disturbance to the clients' therapy. It is difficult to live up to the image of the retiring therapist and probably more useful to recognize the differences and see what can be made of them. When moving from one individual therapist to another the similarities and differences can be tantalizing. The basic principles may be the same but the quality of the experience quite different. The therapy moves between familiar territory and subtle incongruities that have to be accommodated.

It might be helpful for someone who has been in individual therapy to move into group therapy or vice versa. At least then it is obvious that the client is learning a whole new approach. When taking on individuals it is probably wise to err on the side of assuming they are reluctant referees. In fact if the therapist has handled it reasonably well and the client has had a good enough and long enough experience of the retiring therapist they are frequently open to something new.

Inheriting a group

Inheriting a group is an interesting experience. The previous therapist's personality will permeate the group and will highlight how different the new therapist's interactions, expectations and relationships are. A number of the existing group members may bring their therapy to an end and leave with the retiring therapist. The group is depleted, losing not only the therapist but also valued members of the group.

The group culture is deeply embedded, and if the group has a culture of absence or lateness, this can be disturbing to the new therapist and difficult to shift. Respecting the previous therapist helps. It can be wearisome to listen, over some months, to how wonderful she was and by definition how inadequate the impostor therapist is. It would be surprising if there were not some acting out, from either the previous therapist or the group members. It is Sod's Law that they will meet in the local supermarket car park within weeks of the new therapist taking over the group. After a while, bringing in new members with a primary attachment to the new therapist can help the group to come to terms with moving on. It is poignant and moving when a group starts to acknowledge that the new group conductor has something to offer.

Moving a practice

I well remember how furious I was when my therapist announced that she was moving her practice from Central London to somewhere halfway to Croydon. Somehow we managed the transition. Since then I have moved my own practice. So how does one do it with the least disturbance to the therapy?

I think it is important that therapists know what they want and have worked through any ambivalent or guilty feelings about moving. If the therapist is moving to a place where she will feel more secure, the therapy will almost certainly benefit. Of course sometimes moves are outside the control of therapists and the therapist is pushed out into inferior accommodation. This is difficult to deal with. The therapist experiences the same feelings of being pushed around, disrespected and undervalued as the clients. Disentangling whose feelings are whose becomes complicated and the therapist can easily start to feel impotent. Good supervision, where the therapist can give voice to and understand her feelings, will help to hold the whole experience.

With a planned move, timing is of the essence – giving people enough time to adjust to the change but not dragging it out. If too much notice is given it starts to feel like the therapy is only going through the motions because that was what was agreed. Knowing something is ending means it is difficult to start new areas of work. Bizarrely, when I moved my practice from Dulwich to Central London almost all the referrals I got in the West End were people who worked in town and lived near Dulwich. In that case I was moving from low overheads to high overheads and I had to decide how much I would absorb the difference and when I could reasonably put the fees up. The setting influences a client's experience of me and it takes a while to settle and re-establish the therapeutic alliance.

Similar difficulties arise if one changes the time of an analytic group. There may not be room for negotiation, or it may be discussed in the group as something that needs to happen and the group consulted over which alternative times might best suit. It is interesting to note that if the suggestions are discussed in the group a good time seems to emerge.

Locums

Therapy is a demanding profession with limited flexibility. It is important that therapists take a career break at a point where they need one, whether it is for personal, family or career reasons. Therapists can meet their needs while sustaining the practice by using a locum. I have developed real confidence that a good locum can be effective, from my experience of being a locum, using a locum and supervising locums. Of course it means the therapist letting go and trusting the locum. It also means the locum respecting the process and resisting the inclination to make an impact.

Each client in a practice can be treated in a different way and while some will need regular sessions, others may wish to see a locum for occasional support, and some might take the chance to see how they get on alone for a while or have their own sabbatical. The goodwill of a number of colleagues can be drawn upon and clients referred to the particular therapist most likely to meet their needs. It is an opportunity to play with the gender or the orientation and approach of the therapist.

It is easier to use a locum with a group. The 'group' still exists even if the therapist goes away. When I brought a male therapist in as a locum for a group it brought out quite different dynamics in the group, which enabled the group to see different dimensions to the members' personalities. I assume this was because the transference relationships to a male therapist were different. I was not entirely ready to let go and trust the locum but since the locum went for supervision with the therapist who had been supervising my work with the group, some of my anxieties were assuaged. Choosing a locum was tricky. It was tempting to find a senior or well-known colleague. However, I decided it was better to choose someone whose work I knew and who I would feel comfortable sharing the group with. The locums I used were essentially good listeners who would pick up any acting out and deal with it quietly and thoughtfully. I also thought they were people who would be open with me, when I came back, about what had gone on.

Acting as a locum feels an honour and a responsibility. It is useful to know something about the clients; however, one cannot expect to understand what is communicated in real depth. The locum is there as a symbol of the absent therapist and her wish that the group should continue meeting and working. It is a privilege to be invited into clients' lives and sit with them while they work. The locum therapist needs to be sufficiently present that the clients do not become paranoid or burdened by her, and then find a comfortable way to be with the group. The group members will be interested in what the therapist thinks and may want to be validated by her. It is rather like being asked to baby-sit for some children who are old enough to look after themselves but who, if left for too long, would not be able to resist the temptation to get out of order and fight amongst themselves.

Chapter 2

Clinical predicaments

While we strive to provide our clients with a good enough therapeutic experience, the therapy does not always proceed smoothly and we find ourselves faced with difficult clinical situations. Responding to the aftermath of a completed suicide, supporting clients who become ill, perhaps mortally, and terminating inappropriate therapy are situations that require considerable thought and skill on the part of the therapist and can threaten her reputation if not handled well.

Understanding suicidal impulses

My experience of suicide came rather early in my career, when some-one I was training killed himself. He did it in a quiet self-contained way on an anniversary, which produced minimal repercussion for me personally. I wasn't able to feel that anything I could have done would have made any difference. I did wonder why he had started training and whether I had let him down by talking so little about suicide.

Later I was involved with a serious attempt, which was much more disturbing. One way of understanding suicide is that a person attempts suicide in order to kill the unbearable psychic pain inside him. He can-not see any other way of dealing with it. The only way to kill the pain is to kill himself. Of course feelings that require such a violent act are not so easily disposed of. The unbearable feelings frequently transfer to those who are left behind, through a process of projective identifi-cation. Rob Hale (1991) has written helpfully and comprehensively about suicidal acts.

Therapists are used to being on the receiving end of projections but these extreme feelings can be particularly difficult to metabolize. Careful attention to what the therapist is left feeling will reveal which unmanageable feelings have been evacuated into the therapist. In my case, while I might have expected to feel rage or despair at the attempted suicide, what I identified was feeling helpless in the face of what had happened. Eventually I realized that an abusive dynamic had come into play. The client had made sure I could not help him. My hands were metaphorically tied behind my back and then, in fantasy, I was forced to watch him act out his self-destructiveness. I was left feeling helpless in the face of his self-destructiveness. Since this was precisely how *he* felt, he had eloquently allowed me to understand his feelings. The question was whether he had destroyed my capacity to think. Once I understood the dynamic, the feelings that I had internalized lifted and I had the bizarre physical sensation of a weight off my shoulders. I was then able to talk with the client about it. In the event of a completed suicide we are deprived of the opportunity to return the digested feelings but it is just as essential to ensure they do not become lodged in the therapist.

Completed suicide

If we practise for any length of time the chances are that we will have to deal with a serious attempted suicide or a completed suicide. It is difficult to be prepared for the emotional turmoil that ensues but it helps if it can be seen as something that goes with the territory rather than a personal failure.

Unexpected breaks are probably a prime time for suicidal behaviour. Where the pain of abandonment is unbearable a suicide attempt may follow to blot out the abandonment. A therapist who becomes ill or pregnant and requires time away from the client cannot be there for them and the client may act out the annihilation. Linda Anderson (1994) describes how, when she was pregnant, a borderline client killed himself during the break. He found it difficult to look at his fantasies about the intruding baby in anything other than a concrete way and became stuck between the wish for a child and a self-destructive envy. While personal circumstances precipitated the act, it seems likely that his feelings about the break and the baby highlighted his already persecuted isolation.

Our reactions to suicide are not always what we would expect and it can be reassuring to know that others have had similar responses. A *Special Scar: The Experiences of People Bereaved by Suicide*

(Wertheimer, 2001) is a useful book in which people who have been bereaved by suicide describe their experience of attending the inquest, the particular difficulties of the funeral, how they faced suicide as a family, the impact on them and how they sought and used support in the wider world. Any therapist who is bereaved in a similar way by a completed suicide will recognize much of what is described.

Coroner's Court

When a client dies the Coroner's Court has the task of deciding the cause of death. They need information and may well approach a therapist to ask for it. What they are interested in is the last person to see the client in different settings. However, whether you could have managed a crisis in therapy differently is not their concern. They are interested in what happened. Therapists I have interviewed describe how helpful the coroner's officer (usually a police officer) was in understanding the therapist's anxieties and their loss. The officer conveyed to the therapist that it was something that happened and that the coroner was looking to understand what had happened, not to find a scapegoat.

Answering questions at a Coroner's Court may well be part of the process. It is helpful if someone who is used to the process – as many consultant psychiatrists are – can do it. It is unusual to be called to give evidence, but if you are, there is advice available on evidence giving which can enable you to do so more confidently. Generally the advice when attending any court is to address your comments to the judge. You can stand facing the judge and when asked questions turn to the counsel asking the questions before turning back to the judge. Preparation is important. You need to be confident of your facts and know what it is that you want the court to hear. If you have a point of view or an argument that you want to get across it needs to be clear in your own mind. The answer to any question needs to use facts to illustrate the picture you are concerned the court should grasp. Deciding beforehand what you want the court to take away from your evidence will clarify your thinking and enable the court to get the best from you.

The coroner's brief is to ascertain the identity of the deceased and how, when and where they died. The full inquest may not be held for several months and waiting can inhibit the grieving process and prolong the anxiety for a therapist. It is a very public scrutiny of personal tragedy and both the public and the press may attend. The coroner decides how much of the written evidence will be read out in court. It is a formal procedure and witnesses can be cross-examined. Families, who go to the inquest for answers, or to feel heard, can be disappointed by the limited scope of the inquest. The reporting in the local paper can also be hurtful where small details are wrongly reported or blown up out of proportion. Bereaved families respond in a variety of ways. Some simply want to know what happened and find some reconciliation; others may be looking for someone to blame. Guarding one's professional reputation can occasionally become a priority.

Supervision

As a supervisor or manager we owe a duty of care to colleagues in this situation. This may mean 'carrying the can' for what has happened. The last thing someone needs, at a time like this, is a senior colleague who will step sideways out of the firing line. A therapist, who was feeling a failure on learning of a completed suicide, described how helpful it was to have a supervisor who could keep it in proportion and find time to talk about other issues as well. The supervisor is holding the therapist and trying to learn from the situation.

Suicide, which involves evacuating the feelings, is an attack on thinking and can initially undermine the therapist. Therapists rely on linking their thinking and feelings to manage the unmanageable. Suicide is an aggressive concrete intrusion, which it is difficult to come to terms with. A supervisor can help the therapist to distinguish her own feelings from those that the client has evacuated into her. I find it helpful to use Winnicott's ideas, in his 1947 paper 'Hate in the countertransference', to hate the client's boundarylessness (Winnicott, 1975). Both the supervisor and the therapist are trying to digest what has happened. They need to identify the split-off elements that are thrown up and can so easily be swallowed whole by the therapist.

A clear objective assessment of whether each step was taken at the time in good faith and professionally will help therapists to learn from the experience about the professional procedures followed. Carefully reviewing each step of the therapy will reveal areas where things could have been done differently but will often reveal just how well the client was taken care of. Linda Anderson (1994) in her article wonders whether, with hindsight, she could have provided more external support. Providing support that clients will actually use is difficult. Anyone other than the therapist can be experienced as a poor substitute, rather like losing one's mother and being fobbed off with the babysitter. Also, in providing extra support one can feed into the client's sense of shame and inadequacy.

When a suicide is unexpected, a therapist can be left trying to understand what happened, looking for clues. Trying to fit missing pieces together can evoke a sort of madness and distress in the therapist and help is needed to think about what happened. If there are aspects of merging, and fears of survival, that overlap in the therapist's unconscious, it can be difficult for the therapist to separate and understand who the therapist is and who the client is. Searching for missing clues is part of a normal grieving process but the therapist may also be experiencing unconscious resonance, such as trying to communicate with an internalized absent, depressed or dead mother. Thinking about the analytic meaning of feelings evoked by suicide can diffuse the dread of difficult feelings and help in working through them.

In the case of a group client, the therapist may have to tell other clients the news of the suicide. One therapist was left wondering about whether to tell her client group even though the client had left the group, and had not been in it for nine months. The therapist's pondering about whether to tell the group can be explained by understanding suicide as something in the social environment that is so deeply disturbing that it can impinge on the countertransference feelings of the therapist. If a client has attempted suicide at a time that coincided with the therapist's absence, the therapist may become more concerned than usual about being seen as uncommunicative with her clients. Of course the reverberations last for a long time, but it does relieve the therapist of any omnipotent fantasies. It instils in the therapist a real sense of respect for unconscious processes and just how unmanageable feelings can be.

Winnicott wrote: 'There will be suicides, management committees must learn to reconcile themselves to suicide, to truancy, and the occasional maniacal outburst with something in it very like murder, broken windows and destruction of things. Psychiatrists who are blackmailed by these disasters are unable to do what is best for the rest of the community in their care' (Winnicott, 1979: 245).

Terminating inappropriate therapy

Therapists are vulnerable to disturbed clients. The assessment cannot always be accurate. Severe pathology can remain hidden and emerge once the therapeutic relationship has been established. Examples would be those liable to acting out, stalking or inappropriate sexual obsession. The question then becomes: 'How do you terminate the therapy?'

When the therapist is at risk

In one-to-one work the most urgent pressure comes when a practitioner feels at risk from inappropriate sexual advances from clients, or threats of violence and other abuses of the relationship. It is advisable to seek good supervision and report the incident. Stalking and attacks on the property and person of practitioners have been known and in such circumstances the police community protection unit provide useful support.

Where there is no insight and the 'as if' element is lost, it will be necessary to terminate the therapeutic relationship and refer on for a form of treatment that does not engage the transference. A client who is titillating towards the therapist and trying to engage them in a sexual encounter rather than a therapeutic relationship will need to be informed that they are being offered a professional, and not a personal, relationship. Practitioners are sometimes flattered by the interest and an element of self-delusion can follow. Given the intensity associated with erotic transference and countertransference, it may be that not enough attention is paid to it in training and continuing professional development. This leaves practitioners with a sense that erotic countertransference is unmanageable and unfamiliar and may be best not talked about.

There are at least two pitfalls in thinking about risks to the therapist: denial and omnipotence. Denial is in operation when the therapist is not hearing the reality in what the client is saying and naively puts it all down to fantasy which will not be acted on. Omnipotent fantasies take over when the therapist trusts the client and herself to manage whatever is thrown up, without fully realizing the consequences for the therapist, who may have to live with them for years. In the transference, clients occasionally frighten the therapist by revealing an aspect of themselves of which they are frightened. I think it is the familiarity with this that can blind a therapist to the exceptional occasion when she needs to take note and take steps to protect herself.

It is a matter of judgement, influenced by the context and the existing nature of the relationship, whether ending is best done quickly in a matter of fact way or by working towards a diminution of the transference. What is invaluable in these circumstances is not just the supervisor but also known and trusted colleagues who will not jump to reassure or judge, but to whom one can say, 'Let me put this to you'; a thoughtful discussion can follow without any compromise of confidentiality.

Clients sometimes try to continue in treatment inappropriately and the client has difficulty in hearing that psychodynamic treatment has reached its limits. In these circumstances it may be important to stick to the therapy model, avoid providing other forms of gratification, and work to a point where the client wishes to leave. This is not as simple as it sounds. The therapeutic relationship can be very seductive.

Terminating therapy in a group situation

Occasionally someone joins a group and then it becomes apparent that the analytic model is not appropriate to their needs. The therapist then has to help them understand this and work towards their leaving the group. It is extraordinarily complex because the other members may only have a shadowy understanding of the difficulties and may identify with the client and feel guilty that they cannot help. Normally one could expect the group to help the departing member manage the transition. However, it is more complex when the member wishes to stay and is being asked to leave because therapy is inappropriate.

Tempting as it may be, it is important not to draw attention to the client's pathology or how they have behaved, but rather to illustrate why it is inappropriate for them to stay. It can be containing for clients to have clear boundaries imposed in a respectful way. The difficulty is to resist telling them in a way that invites escalation. One runs the risk of humiliating the client and splitting the group. The key issue is that the therapist is certain that psychodynamic treatment is inappropriate and therefore it would be unprofessional as well as unwise to continue.

It is the therapist's professional responsibility to convey this to the client. It may involve acknowledging that the therapist made a mistake in selecting the client for treatment. The language used will influence the result and it is helpful if it can convey clarity, respect, kindness and professionalism. There is always a risk of suicide or other acting out; however, if one can be straight with clients, give a clear leaving date and help them manage the leaving, they have the opportunity for a containing holding experience alongside the rejection.

Legal action

Where the experience has become delusional and the client refuses to accept that the relationship has ended, a situation not unlike stalking can develop. In the last resort, it may be necessary to apply to the courts for a restraining order. This is a difficult decision for a therapist to take. If the client is unable to comply he will ultimately be before the courts on an imprisonable offence. It is also very expensive for the therapist who, while she may eventually be able to reclaim the costs from the client, has to find the substantial lawyer's fees in the first instance.

Clients who become terminally ill

I had the misfortune over a short period to take on a number of apparently healthy individuals who became ill and died while in therapy. Colleagues have found themselves in similar situations. It is not as uncommon as we would like to think, particularly if the therapist sees the larger number of clients involved in group therapy. My experience was in a group setting. The dynamics of working individually with a client who is seriously ill or dying may be different from a group, but each of my clients was an individual to me. I was simply seeing them in a context where other people also participated. I hope that those who only work with individuals will be able to make the connection to their own setting.

Therapists normally work with the inner world and are careful not to give advice or engage in the real world of their clients. When real events intrude into the therapy they are seen as grist to the mill. However, this relies on incorporating any event into the fantasy world of the therapy. I am not sure that serious illness and death can be managed in exactly this way. One can still look at the fantasies but it is difficult to play with them in the face of the reality in the room. How does the therapist respond to a reality such as illness or death intruding into this fantasy world and how can it be addressed?

Serious illness

Therapy provides a space where the unthinkable can be thought. The client does not have to protect the therapist in the way he might wish to protect his family. Therapy can also provide a container for the 'unbearable'. If unmanageable feelings, impulses and circumstances can be addressed once or twice a week, the time in between may be less fraught. A client who knows what it is that he thinks and feels is less likely to be fragmented and vulnerable. Information he has been given elsewhere can be usefully thought about and processed in the therapy session. Questions that lurk at the back of the mind can take shape and be put into words, which allows them to be thought about.

Pain

Each illness brings its own constellation of anxieties and persecutory aspects. The management of symptoms and the side effects of treatment can be a real focus of concern. It is difficult to sit with people who are in physical pain and it can be difficult for them to tolerate our losing sight of the pain they are in, both physical and psychological. The experience of pain we draw on is often from the early childhood experience of others who were in excruciating pain. It is easy to discount the advances in medication and collude with a fear that the pain cannot be managed either by the patient or by the doctors. While a pain clinic can be a useful resource, a therapist who bridges the gap between the medical and the psychological by being there, sharing the pain and the rage, is also valuable.

Anxiety

Lowering anxiety is thought to decrease pain and this might be one contribution a therapist can make by exploring the anxieties. Clients will be concerned about the effect of the illness on their family and there may be real financial worries. They may be caught up in collusive, mutually protective behaviour, which prevents honest discussion with their family and results in increasing withdrawal and isolation. It is difficult to resist the basic instinct to protect our family from bad news but, on the whole, having the information and being able to talk together provides better support. Some clients need help with asserting their needs to the medical profession, others may need to look at developing an appropriate level of trust that allows the medical professionals to share the responsibility and care for them.

It can be helpful for the therapist, without breaking confidentiality, to talk to a medical practitioner about the likely course of the particular illness. Progressive neurological diseases are particularly difficult to deal with because loss follows loss. If the illness causes difficulties with speech or body control, understanding one another can prove difficult.

When a client dies

As a therapist we have an unparalleled opportunity to learn about those aspects of life that we may face in the future. Death is the one event we can all rely on experiencing. When a client leaves therapy, this often evokes memories of loss and bereavement, which can be used to talk about death and dying. However, being a therapist or a member of a group while another member is really dying is not easy, and after three totally unexpected deaths in as many years I have tried to describe the experience and the sense I have made of it.

Train crash parallel

My initial experience of managing this intrusion of reality into the analytic space was that I wished we were in my colleague's office in the palliative care department where painful deterioration, death and dying really are all grist to the mill. It reminded me of what hospital staff describe after a disaster. Doctors and nurses describe an experience of having demonstrated what they were capable of, and a sense of doing something useful. They regret that others had to suffer to provide the opportunity, and are glad it is over. More disturbed are those who find themselves outside the context of their usual area of competence. They stood by unable to do anything practical and were only able to talk to and comfort those injured. Our clients bring us traumatic events week in and week out which we deal with like the doctors and nurses. However, there are occasional, exceptional cases where circumstances conspire together to put us in the same position as the clerical worker who, while she played a vital psychological role, was not able to change the course of events and found herself in a mangled carriage, feeling inadequate.

Terminal diagnosis

When an apparently healthy client joins a group for one of the usual reasons, the work starts, transferences are built up and a shared fantasy is indulged in. When such a client receives a terminal diagnosis and looks to me for help with the reality of their life I am in a situation not unlike that of the receptionist in the crumpled carriages. I sit there knowing that we are experiencing and reflecting the inner world of the client and his family but that there is also a powerful reality, which we must confront. Therapists and groups usually work by resonating together. What seems unbearably complex and unmanageable slowly changes and evolves into a pattern that can be integrated into the psyche. This requires a level of mutual association. The problem is that dying is essentially something we do alone, with the help of our friends. Our secular society has a woefully inadequate vocabulary for death, which leaves clients struggling.

Being there for someone who is dying

There is a wish to put life on hold when someone is dying, but it is neither desirable nor possible. It is important for the therapist to ensure all members of a group continue to feel that their needs are valid and that the group can be trusted to deal with whatever evolves. Can someone whose parent is dying bring this into a group that is dealing with a dying member? Can the group truly be there for him when his parent dies or is it all too painful? Can grieving with him help the dying member grieve for his own mortality? Groups can easily get caught up in magical thinking. Someone in a group where two people have died could easily get caught up in the fantasy that he would be the next to die.

We like to delude ourselves that we are immortal. Having to face the reality of our own mortality is not always welcome. One way clients can avoid working with death is by splitting and setting up a false dichotomy, which precludes real work. In a group this might crystallize out as one member denying that the situation is serious whilst another is already planning the funeral. One element might retreat into denial and the other into fatalistic acceptance. Each can then attack the other and avoid really thinking about what it means. On the other hand death is at the heart of much therapeutic work, and group members more familiar with death can provide pearls of wisdom, which help everyone negotiate this difficult terrain.

A client's personality structures and previous experience of death will influence his response to his illness in the group. The way he tells the group and the underlying message he conveys about the help he needs are particularly important. A client who has always had to rely on himself and protect his parents may have enormous difficulty in bringing himself to tell the group. Clients are fearful of overloading a group when there is nothing the group can do to help, and clients may delay telling the group. It is not unusual for a client to say the important things at the end of the group and if he is unable to come back it leaves the group struggling.

The client will make his own informed judgement about what the group or therapist is willing to struggle with. It is likely he will be angry about why this should have happened to him and question whether his life has meant anything to anyone. Those with a religious belief need to be able to share their lapses of faith and not feel their basic faith will be taken away from them. Can the group or the therapist be trusted with fears around the unknown, annihilation and death? For some the process of dying is the focus, for others it is death itself. These feelings move and change as the process unfolds. Regrets from the past, wanting to be reconciled and leaving everything in order can become preoccupations that may need real attention.

What a client tells the therapist about their illness will also communicate something about their early experience. The therapist is left to digest this along with the difficult news. The therapy group may regress and its priority shift to survival rather than analysis. The sudden impingement of reality can mean defensive structures come to the fore and the group's usual mode of communication through mirroring and resonance may be limited. Clearly the group and the therapist only know what the members bring to the group. Group members are more likely to withhold difficult feelings from the therapist at a time like this and there will be issues that do not get addressed. This could lead to someone dropping out, or an internal suspension of the therapy, but one hopes the treatment alliance will be resumed later.

Rosemary Burch has written an as yet unpublished paper, 'What happens in a group when all the members know they are dying' (personal communication). She suggests it might be helpful to run groups for clients with advanced cancer on the basis of a nine-month year. This would give the therapist a chance to metabolize the difficult feelings raised in the group, and would also give the group an opportunity to work towards a planned ending that is not death. Thus issues of abandonment, separation, grief and loss can be worked with in the group (Burch, 2000).

Death in the inner and outer world

Many of our clients have had traumatic bereavements, which we would usually work through in time. To have death, both in the real present and in the inner world, may be too much, and appropriate defence mechanisms such as splitting and denial come into play. One can imagine one client refusing to believe things really are as serious as they seem, while another over-identifies with the dying client. In either case the therapist has to address herself to the question of whether it is better addressed in the here and now or as transference.

The relationships our clients have with one another, and with us, are a mass of transference relationships, which are either thrown into relief or concretized when such a powerful dose of reality is introduced. It is one thing to fantasize that you have a special relationship with another group member, quite another to find yourself confided in about a fatal illness. One purpose of a group is to provide a safe place where transference relationships can be explored, and differences and misunderstandings are lived through. However, where the relationship is cut short through illness or death there is a danger that any negative transference becomes concretized. Groups are like families and it would not be surprising if a member loyally continued whatever feud the dying member had been engaged in. As with families it is the things we said, and did not say, that come back to haunt us. It is also worth noting how groups start to behave like families, fighting over who knew what the person who died would have wanted.

With a well-selected analytic group I usually feel confident that I have all the resources I need to deal with whatever the group throws up. The personality of the person who is dying and their approach to their illness is what is going to determine what is needed from the group. Illness is a bodily function, and how the client and the group feel about their bodies will be central to what can be talked about. One of the main complaints from anyone who is ill is the sense of losing their privacy, and feeling that their body has become public property. The therapist has an important role in protecting the vulnerable client from further intrusion. Equally, being able to talk about the reality of what is happening can be an invaluable support. The lasting memory I have of one of my clients who died was of the beautiful head wrap she had created and which we and she took pleasure in.

The non-attending group member

Once someone can no longer attend the therapy through illness, the relationship with the therapist has to be negotiated. I kept up some contact but I have colleagues who took the line that this was the end of the relationship and maintained an analytic clarity. Keeping in touch by card or telephone is not difficult for a while. However, as an illness progresses, communication can become more difficult and the therapist becomes dependent on the goodwill of the family, who are themselves distressed.

If the group member who develops symptoms and becomes ill is in the group as part of a training requirement, the course itself can provide support to both the therapist and the client. When the client is no longer able to come to the group he remains part of a larger group, the network of friends, course staff and students, and work colleagues who if necessary can form an extended family and help him die well. The course staff have a different level of contact with the student therapist and can help to hold the group by keeping in touch with the therapist in a way that respects the various boundaries. Where they are invited by the family, the therapist and those members of the group who wish to, may go to the funeral. It places the death in the real world where it needs to be. The therapist has support, information, time to mourn and an opportunity to make sense of what has happened.

It is of course even more difficult when someone lacks the social support of a family and lives alone. If a group member fails to return after a break the therapist may find herself in the position of having to phone the GP or local hospice only to discover that the client died while the therapist was away. In my experience people die as they have lived. Those who have lived independently die independently, in spirit at least.

When someone is ill, membership is complex. With a dying client the therapist is invited into a world she is usually excluded from, the real world of the client. A mindful therapist will be aware of the extra dynamic this introduces into the therapy. The therapeutic relationship is not well designed to support this level of complexity. I think of giving birth and dying as essentially similar experiences where a midwife is needed to facilitate the transition. It is an extraordinary privilege to be with someone who is dying.

Section 2

What can a therapist learn from business ideas?

Practice development (*Michael Wilkins*)
Business planning – key steps to plan your practice
A development plan
Financial planning
Competition
Partnership practices
A budget
Service development
Conclusion

Money
How much can we expect to earn?
Unconscious attitudes towards money
Negotiating fees
When the client fails to pay
Managing the finances

Marketing your skills
Overcoming inhibitions about marketing
Forming referral networks
Teaching, cards and websites;
Promoting your therapy service

Time management
Conceptualizing time
Managing the paperwork
Using routine to provide structure
Managing ourselves
Procrastination is the thief of time
Rewarding ourselves

Why is it called 'Free Association' when its' so expensive?

Cartoon by Mel Calman. © S. and C. Calman.

Chapter 3
Practice development

Michael Wilkins

Think about how you are developing your practice. How do you decide whether to move in one direction or another? Simple planning can help you extend your practice so that it provides the required income and interest. Applying basic tools from small business management will pave the way for a substantial practice based on quality work.

Those in the world of therapy, and other professional practices, do not always take easily to the idea of being a business. Somehow it detracts from the personal service we are offering and suggests commercialism and profit. Our choice of profession is linked to a number of aspects about our values and ourselves. Many therapists come from a health, education or social services setting and bring with them expectations and assumptions that have developed in those cultures. These underpin much of the solid foundations of a therapy practice. However, we are practising our therapy skills in order to provide an income, and a glance at some of the ideas developed in running small businesses might pay dividends.

Business planning – key steps to plan the practice

Research suggests that those who plan are more likely to succeed. Developing and extending a practice entails thinking through what you want to achieve. There are different forms of business planning, ranging from a simple development plan that outlines the areas you want to develop and how to achieve these developments, to detailed financial planning that you would show to a bank or financial institution when looking for finance. Pulling the following three steps together leads to a plan to develop the practice:

- *Clarifying your vision* – this drives planning. It is what you want the work to look like in the future to meet your dreams.
- *Understanding your present practice* – it is useful to know where you are starting from and what the structure of the practice is today.
- *Analysing strengths and weaknesses (SWOT analysis)* – this structures some thinking about what strengths you have and areas that could be seen as weaker. Add to that the opportunities you have and any threats to your practice.

Envisaging the future

Planning starts with the vision you have of what you want to achieve financially, professionally and personally through work. What is important to you in working as a therapist? How busy do you want to be in three years' time? What times of the day do you want to work? It might be creative to revisit the question of why you are doing the kind of work you are doing, as part of a regular review. The work a therapist enjoys changes over the years, as circumstances and life stages change. A therapist with young children will be subject to different constraints from one who is celebrating the children leaving home. Gladeana McMahon (1994) in her excellent book, *Setting Up Your Own Private Practice: in Counselling and Psychotherapy*, looks at how a therapist can think about the kind of practice that will meet her needs and how a therapist can manage the shift from part-time to full-time practice.

A clearer vision will emerge through looking at different aspects of the work:

- How much income needs to be generated this year and in the future?
- How many years do you see yourself continuing to practise?
- What is your desired lifestyle? Will this allow you to work evenings or weekends?
- Are there talents you would like to develop or use that are dormant?
- What are your continuing professional development priorities?
- Would you like to develop a practice with others or buy a property to operate from?

Your vision will inform the detail of your planning. It begins to define the boundaries for the type of practice you need to develop to fulfil your vision. You can also check that any plans you make will help you achieve the vision. It can help too with decision-making when opportunities arise. If you are wondering whether you want to take an opportunity that has arisen then refer back and see how it would help you achieve your vision.

An example of a vision is: 'In 5 years I want to be running a sole practice with a turnover of £45K p.a. with the income broken down into 70% therapy (80% individual, 20% group), 20% supervision and 10% teaching. I only want to work four days and two evenings a week.'

Analysing the current practice

Once a vision has been clarified a good next step is to analyse the present practice. The purpose of this analysis is to understand the make-up of the existing practice so that changes can be planned. One way to do this is to pull out the different aspects of the practice under headings. The following are examples of key headings you could use to break down the practice; however, it is not exhaustive.

1. Clinical clients

- What fee levels (how many under each level?).
- Issues they bring (how many under each issue?).
- Length of contract (how many will be with you for how long?).
- How often you see them (once/twice a week?).

2. Income streams (the percentage of income from each activity)

- From individuals.
- From groups.
- From supervision you offer.
- From teaching.

3. Number of organizations (such as training institutes) that you work for and the percentage of your income from each.

4. Referrers

- Type of referrer, e.g. GPs, colleague, institutes.

- Numbers of clients referred by each.
- Type of referrals from each referrer, e.g. what clinical issues, gender, etc.

With this information you can assess how each part of the practice leads towards the vision. Then decisions can be made as to which parts need to be built up, run down or maintained at the present level.

SWOT analysis

Another useful measure, having analysed your existing business, is to undertake a SWOT analysis (Figure 3.1). SWOT stands for strengths, weaknesses, opportunities and threats.

The first two categories refer to your practice; strengths refers to the aspects of your practice that you see as positive in achieving your vision, and weaknesses are those that can be seen as militating against the achievement of your vision. Opportunities and threats are the aspects outside your practice that you may have limited control over, but highlight how the environment surrounding your practice may aid or militate against the achievement of your vision.

Strengths	Weaknesses
■ Accredited by BACP & UKCP Reg.	■ Limited supervisory experience
■ Good contact with three local GPs	■ Not teaching at present (not sure who is running courses at my institute as I have lost contact)
■ Trained by well-respected body	
■ 70% of clients pay top fees	■ Few referrers (mainly GPs)
■ Have had one supervisory client	
■ Good contacts in NHS	
Opportunities	**Threats**
■ Growing market for psychotherapy from GPs	■ More competitors in area
■ Counselling and psychotherapy more accepted	■ People looking for short-term interventions rather than long-term
■ Impact of ageing population, early retirement as opportunity for market to enter	■ Recession hitting incomes
	■ Cognitive behavioural therapy more popular

Figure 3.1 **An example of a SWOT analysis**

A development plan

With a clear vision, a SWOT analysis and the analysis of your present practice you are in a good position to plan the development of your practice. Planning is a punctuation in the process of life. 'Where am I now and where do I want to get to?' The development plan is one view of how to get there using what is known today. Tomorrow may bring feedback or an opportunity that means the plan needs to be revised. A good plan should have alterations as time goes on; it is not something set in stone. A development plan such as the one shown in Figure 3.2 (begun, but not completed) would be suitable for many practitioners. The timescales and resource requirements should be realistic and the outcomes should be specific and measurable.

Once a development plan has been created it can be used to decide on a marketing strategy, which will implement the plan. The chapter on 'Marketing your skills' (Chapter 5) considers the issues of marketing in more detail but, essentially, successful marketing tends to be targeted. Knowing where to target is related to the work you have done on the present status of your practice and the vision you have for where you want it to be. It may be you need to target a specific client group or particular professionals who may become referrers. You may wish to offer a new service such as supervision. Experience suggests that if a new service is to be offered then where possible enter it somewhere you already hold credibility. An alternative development is to take your existing skills into a new marketplace. Doing both – developing a new service and entering into a new market at the same time – is difficult as it means building credibility in both the service and the marketplace. The chapter 'Working in different settings' (Chapter 7) describes some of the challenges involved in diversifying as a therapist.

Financial planning

If your practice is bringing in finances at a level that meets your costs and enables you to live, then financial planning may be less of an issue. However, if part of your planning is to increase your income, then financial planning will be important. The chapter in this book on 'Money' (Chapter 4) deals with finance in more detail. For an individual practitioner there are a number of ways of increasing your income.

Vision: in 5 years I want to be running a sole practice with a turnover of £45,000 p.a. with the income broken down into 70% psychotherapy (80% individual, 20% group), 20% supervision and 10% teaching. I only want to work four days and two evenings a week.

This year to raise income to £35,000; add more supervision contracts to 10% of income and to include teaching in my practice.

Aspect of vision	Development	Actions	When by	Resources required	Success criteria
Add to income and raise percentage of supervisory contracts	(1) To increase number of supervisory contracts	(a) Contact institute to discuss possibility of supervising students (b) Investigate registration as a supervisor with BACP (c) Act on it if I meet criteria (d) Devise and activate marketing plan for supervision	(a) 1 February (b) 1 March (c) End of March (d) End of April	Time to complete application Cost of marketing material and time to devise plan	(a) Know what I need to do to become a supervisor at the institute (b) Have the information and can act upon it (c) Have applied, if able (d) Marketing plan in operation
Look to increase number of clients and income, broaden base of referrers	(2) Increase number of GPs who refer	(a) Talk with existing GP referrers about other colleagues I could speak to (b) Use my NHS contacts to make new contacts (c) Contact and arrange to meet new possible referrers	(a) End of January (b) End of February (c) End of April	Time	Three new referral sources by end of June
Add training/teaching as an income stream	(3) Become a lecturer on a training course	Choose area of expertise to lecture on and approach course chairs for next year's programme	April	2 days to prepare content 1 day to talk with chairs of courses	Be included on a course programme. If not able to, run a workshop for the institute

Figure 3.2 A development plan for a psychotherapist

- Increase the number of clients; impossible if you are already working all the time you want or can.
- Keep the number of clients the same but look for referrals at a higher fee level.
- Increase your fees all round.
- Increase the proportion of the type of service that brings in better returns; e.g. do you earn more for supervision or for therapy clients?

Planning changes in your practice can cost, if not money, then time when you could be earning. Therapists suffer from the 'feast or famine' syndrome. It is difficult to find time to network or market when you have sufficient referrals but then the referrals can begin to dry up as people think you are full and it is hard work to build the level up again. Keeping a time for networking and marketing is always advisable in order to try and reduce the impact of this roller coaster.

Competition

If the number of practising therapists is increasing and the number of people wanting the service that therapists offer is becoming static, careful planning will be essential to maintain the practice at the required level. Those in business constantly face these issues. Any new product or service they introduce is swiftly copied or developed by someone else and the number of consumers requiring the product or service reaches a limit. Take for example the mobile telephone industry, which has grown to a point where the manufacturers are finding that they cannot continue to sell new handsets at the rate that they have been doing. This has led to loss of jobs within the industry and loss of income. The industry is facing a shakedown and will need to find different avenues to increase the income into the industry. This may include developing new services such as 3G. Something similar may soon be happening within the therapy world. Ideas from the commercial business world could aid established practising therapists in continuing to be successful and build practices at a time when there is more competition for therapy services.

Partnership practices

Private therapists mostly practise within structures that provide some form of network and referral system. There are few structured businesses with therapists directly employed and paid a salary. Most therapists practise independently as sole traders. Increasingly therapists are coming together to form practices. Premises may be bought or rented and used on a cost-sharing basis, which allows the therapists to work collaboratively, or independently in conducting their own practices. Alternatively therapists may simply rent rooms from an established therapist or a complementary therapy centre. Being part of a practice can be expensive but it confers the benefits of visibility, networking and support. *The Practice of Group Analysis* (Roberts and Pines, 1991) describes how one established practice is run.

Other professions such as solicitors and accountants who have become more regulated have found that it has become difficult to survive as individuals or very small partnerships. There have been a number of mergers and increases in size for these practices. Part of the reason for this is the amount of administration that has developed through regulation. This may be the future for therapy. At present there is little regulation, and therefore formal administration, other than for taxation, record keeping and continuing professional development purposes.

A budget

Business planning for existing practices with a steady income stream may not require a major financial component, unless the practice is being developed as a partnership with all income going to the partnership and drawings being made by the partners. In cases like this, budgets and cash flow forecasts need to be considered so that the income coming into the partnership covers the expenses of running the partnership, such as office costs and overheads, as well as the salaries the partners draw. However, it is good practice to consider a budget if you are going to invest in renting property, marketing activity or other costs to develop your practice. The budget may not just be financial; it could be a time budget. If you undertake a major marketing drive, which includes networking etc., it takes time that you are working but not earning. It might be possible to plan to promote the practice for a day a week for three months and then expect to see the benefits of the campaign in the following months through increased earnings.

Service development

Businesses that survive and prosper are constantly reviewing the services that they offer. This is driven in part by the changing perception of needs that people have and also by looking for new opportunities where professional skills can be applied. This is vital for therapy as the marketplace may change and the perception of therapy may also change. The growth of short-term therapy is a challenge for those offering longer-term therapy, as the present culture appears to be driven by a low-attention-span, quick-results orientation. The National Health Service or insurance companies do not always fund the cost of longer-term work. Other ways of using therapy skills are being developed, for example the growth of employee assistance programmes and mentoring in the business world. How do therapists respond to these changes?

The services you offer and how you describe them may need to change in order to meet changing expectations. If you think long-term therapy is required for the problems presented, you will need to be able to explain the value that clients will get from investing the high level of time and money required. Clients easily accept that long-term therapy is something therapists value but there is considerable resistance to the idea that it is the best solution for them. In the long run you can only practise the type of therapy that people are prepared to pay for. Simply changing the language used to describe your approach may enable you to continue doing what you believe in. So, like healthy humans, a therapy practice will need to change and adapt to meet changing circumstances and develop services to meet them.

Conclusion

Thinking of the practice as a business, with all the commercial overtones that this might have, may not come easily to some therapists.

However, in order to survive and prosper, it is advisable to act as a business and consider the issues raised in this chapter. It is essential to have a clear idea of what you want the practice to deliver for you and to formulate constructive plans for how to achieve it. This will facilitate both marketing and the capacity to develop a service which meets changing needs and perceptions.

Chapter 4
Money

A full-time practice, which has to pay the mortgage, will need to find answers to bad debt, tax, clients who challenge fees, and how to value the work we do. An understanding of our own and our clients' relationship with money, alongside good financial advice, will go some way to addressing these issues.

How much can we expect to earn?

Paying for the training

No one who is seriously interested in money becomes a therapist. The training is expensive and usually unsubsidized. The amount a therapist can earn is limited by the number of hours she can work. Perhaps the most depressing exercise is to take the cost of the training, and the hours spent on it, and calculate how long it will take to recoup the investment. Unless a therapist earns a great deal more after training than she would have done in the original profession, it takes a long time. Of course there are rewards other than financial, but knowing how much we have invested in our professional selves can be a spur to finding suitable remuneration. Therapy is a fascinating and moving occupation. Is the aim to make a 'good living' or is it enough merely to cover the 'cost of living'? Would winning the lottery change the fees charged?

Professional fees or pin money

Running a practice is expensive and paying an accountant, or other professional, vast sums of money can be painful. However, the experience confronts us with what other people charge, usually without blinking an eyelid. It is also a useful reminder of what it feels like to be the person paying, however good the service. These professionals appear to have no qualms about charging, while therapists often struggle with how much they can charge. We encourage our clients to get in touch with their envy and, rather than languishing in the slough of resentment, transform it into desire. Maybe properly channelled desire can enable us to get a proper level of remuneration in line with other professionals.

Theoretically, therapists work out what they need to earn, how many clients they expect to see, and charge accordingly. In reality I think most people look at what everyone else is charging and place themselves where they feel comfortable in relation to colleagues. A few therapists with high overheads may charge slightly more but there is no real tradition of experienced therapists charging more than the newly qualified. In part this is because few people in psychotherapy and counselling are truly beginners. Most therapists bring with them skills from an allied profession. There may be some advantages to being a 'senior' therapist and it is probably easier to sustain a practice but the financial reward may not be significantly different.

Generally clients pay what is asked. They mind paying it, and that is grist to the mill in the analytic work. I am not sure how the value of therapy can be quantified. I once worked out how much the income of some clients had increased as a result of therapy. One got a grant to study, another got a job, yet another was promoted, and so on. It added up to an impressive sum. However, my enthusiasm for this simple method of calculating the value of therapy was slightly dimmed when I realized that in another part of my practice women were giving themselves permission to work part-time and men were quitting the city for less well-paid, socially-rewarding employment.

Dependency on fees

Being dependent on the income from therapy is a problem. It is possible to become corrupted by the dependency. A case can be made for saying that clients should not constitute more than a half of a therapist's income. Will a run of dropouts cause problems with the bank or will it just mean that this year's holiday is spent at home? A colleague who had spent years working in tough areas of the voluntary sector understood this dilemma. Wanting to train as a therapist, he first took an unrelated job, involving high pressure selling of financial products. He reasoned this would give him the financial security to afford to train and then to see the clients he wanted to see, rather than the number he would need to see, if he was to survive on the income from therapy alone. Anyone at the point of thinking of giving up the day job would be well advised to give it some careful thought.

Unconscious attitudes towards money

Paying for therapy

As a generalization, those who can well afford therapy often have the greatest difficulty paying for it, while those who have few resources will stretch themselves to meet the fee. One way of understanding this is to realize that there are two approaches to worrying about money. People tend to worry either about how to earn money or about how to limit their expenditure. It is difficult to worry about both. The more affluent high earner finds it hard to pay because he is preoccupied with conserving his capital and focuses on conserving what he is spending. Those who are less well off know that the bills will come in and will have to be paid; their preoccupation is with earning enough to meet the bill.

Childhood relationship to money

Our childhood experiences of money influence the present. A therapist whose father was a farmer might be good at maximizing productivity, while someone with experience of second-hand car sales will know about surviving cash flow problems, and the child of a hospital worker may simply know how to make ends meet. The financial decisions we experience as difficult are often a product of our past experience, rather than something intrinsic.

At a workshop for therapists on 'Money' most of the talk was of how those present had struggled to make ends meet when they were young. The therapists felt guilty about charging clients and found they were doing the work for as little as possible. Far from overcoming my own constraints, as I had hoped, I found them confirmed. I decided that next time I was struggling with a financial issue, I would try to go to a conference for a variety of professionals where I might get some support for the idea that I was a professional, offering a service which people are willing to pay for because they need it and it makes a difference to their lives.

Voluntary work

Therapists from families that valued charitable giving and voluntary work will have a clear grasp of the idea of mutual benefit. The therapist will do some unpaid work for a colleague or a training institute because it will raise her profile and paid work will follow in due course. Voluntary work handled well is one of the most effective marketing strategies. However, occasionally others misread the situation. I was conducting a group alongside a colleague, and referrers knew I was occasionally willing to take a low fee client. I assumed a balance of high fee clients would make up the difference. That was fine until I discovered I was being sent all the low fee clients and another colleague was being sent all the high fee clients. I had to make it clear that if people wanted me to take low fee clients they would also have to send me those who could afford to pay more.

Money as communication

Therapists are in a unique position, trying to be business-like without losing the communication that comes with the fee payment. It is a difficult balance to achieve. It means holding in mind what the money and the communications around it mean. Psychologically, fee payment occurs at the boundary of the relationship between the inner world and the outer world. The communications that go with the payment, rather like the communications in the first and last five minutes of the session, have an added authenticity, which needs to be observed and worked with, though clearly not pounced upon. A therapist will notice the person who pays late, however politely or charmingly, and the person who pays with a disgruntled look. Denied facets of the personality, which are not expressed in the regressed situation of the therapy, can sometimes be glimpsed at the moment of payment. Taken alongside the personal history, it gives an inkling of the client's relationship to the therapy. The client who is used to paying prostitutes can evoke the same response in the therapist who is sensitive to the mutual denigration. Clients who feel they prostitute themselves for money re-enact that relationship with the therapist.

What does the roll of bank notes mean? Is it a way of reducing the payment to petty cash or of showing the therapist that the client can buy anything he wants? Other clients may want to dismiss the financial transaction and maintain the illusion that the therapy is done for love. It was salutary for me to consult a private physiotherapist for a fractured wrist. She was very good but I realized how much I minded paying her. I wanted to cut corners, and was sceptical of how often I needed to go. I said little of this to her. It made me more alert to potential unspoken feelings my clients might have about having to pay.

Money as power

Where the power lies is a complex relationship. Paying could give the client a sense of control and bring some equality into the relationship. However, if the client is unhappy, all he can do is withhold payment and ultimately the therapist will withhold treatment. A child who grandiosely says, 'I'm not going to do what you say', risks not being fed and cared for. The relationship requires the client to have the money to pay for the treatment. How does a therapist deal with the client who cannot pay or will not pay? Clients with a history of fraud may test the boundaries, plausibly asserting that the elusive cheque is in the post. They will need very careful management and may in the final resort have to face the consequences of their actions and be helped to leave therapy with an understanding of why the exploitation cannot be allowed to continue.

Taking on too much work

Therapists need enough money to live on. It is tempting to take on work just because it is there and will pay the mortgage. The difficulty comes when a therapist is talked into taking something on against her better judgement. It is easy to take on work that will not be enjoyable, or even work that requires a different skill base, when an esteemed colleague asks for assistance. Colleagues can be persuasive, saying, 'It is only for 30 sessions', or 'It will not be that demanding'. A therapist who regrets having taken on the work can easily start resenting the client or institution. In such circumstances it becomes increasingly complicated to discern what is going on and get any satisfaction from the work. Where the therapist has optimistically, or desperately, taken on a particularly disturbed client complex repercussions can follow. Simply recognizing that it was a mistake to take the work on can be a relief. Setting limits is important and some ideas are discussed in the chapter on 'Time management' (Chapter 6). Good boundaries around the work engaged in will give some protection from optimistically thinking that of course it can all be fitted in and of course the one remaining evening must be given up for such an interesting venture.

Negotiating fees

The initial session fee

Setting the fee for the initial session is complex. It is the session that requires the greatest professional skill and can take longer than the 50-minute hour. It may also entail correspondence with the GP and referrer. It is not realistic to set a fee which reflects the amount of time and expertise that has gone into the session. If it is too high, it will deter potential clients from coming. Clients frequently assume the initial session will be free. They need to be informed before they come if there will be a fee and some indication of what it might be. Some clients engage in wishful thinking, confusing psychotherapy and counselling with pastoral care, which is available without charge through various organizations. Others have the insurance salesman in mind, who only charges if you decide to go ahead and purchase. If I am interested to see someone but think fees are likely to be an issue I might say what my standard fee is but suggest it is open to negotiation when we meet.

I think of the initial session as an assessment interview. The client is paying for an opinion as to whether psychotherapy would be suitable. There is no obligation on either side. The fee probably needs to be as high as, or more than, the standard fee. It sets the tone of the charges and helps establish whether the client is able and willing to invest what is required in psychotherapy. Essentially one charges what the market will bear and this may vary with location and prevailing opportunities for psychotherapy.

Setting fees

Some therapists have a fee which clients can either meet or not. Others operate a sliding scale where the level of income determines the level of fee paid. An alternative is to have a standard fee, which is set high enough to subsidize one or two clients on a low income. Clients can become unemployed during the course of the therapy and this can then be accommodated. Flexibility introduces negotiation and there will be the occasional misunderstanding. It is not easy for the therapist to find the appropriate response to the low fee client who calmly announces that they will not be able to come next week because they are off to the Seychelles for their holiday.

The issue the client is bringing to therapy can be demonstrated through the money. A client who has had to grow up prematurely and operate as a parentified child, looking after distressed parents, may find it intolerable to admit to any difficulty in meeting the fee the therapist asks. Such clients take pride in meeting the needs of others regardless of the personal cost. If they cannot afford the fees, rather than saying so, they will assure the therapist that they can find the money from somewhere. Of course it is tempting to collude with this, but perhaps more useful to work with it. I have found it helpful on occasion to encourage a client to stay in the uncomfortable position of realizing that he cannot meet my needs by paying the fees and that I cannot meet his needs by reducing the fees far enough. I encourage the client to stay with the very real problem, until we find a way through, rather than omnipotently solving it himself by going away, paying what he cannot afford, or seducing me.

Raising fees

It is helpful if clients know that fees rise annually. If this idea is introduced they expect increases. Gradual increases are usually easier to deal with than sudden hikes in costs. Round figures are more acceptable than percentage increases, which can irritate clients. Initially the increase is probably best simply announced. Negotiation may follow if clients choose to or need to take it up. It is worth keeping an eye on the market. As an experienced therapist it is easy to let fees slide downwards in relation to others. New therapists set their fees at the going rate. It is notable how often I have discovered that slothfulness has resulted in my fees slipping below those charged elsewhere, by less experienced colleagues. If one is influenced by the adage 'What you get is what you pay for', it soon starts to look as if these colleagues are providing the more valuable therapy.

Fees in the context of an analytic group

Each mode of therapy has its own relationship with money and the part it plays in the therapy. A systemic therapist is likely to attach less importance to who is paying for a young person's therapy than an analytically trained individual therapist. A group analyst has to think whether the contract a member enters into is with the group or the therapist and how payment and non-payment of fees is to be processed by the therapist and the group. If the financial contract is seen to be between the therapist, whose income depends on it, and the individual members, can the issues still be brought into the group? Payment to therapists will reflect changes in the wider community. Clients are likely to try to negotiate a fee or want a cashless solution such as a direct debit. I think it is a mistake simply to interpret these as resistances in the client.

Fee-paying is a direct physical exchange in a process otherwise ruled by verbal, symbolic exchanges. Fluctuations in fee-paying are usually analysed in terms of resistance, defence mechanisms, transference and symbolic interaction. Interpreting individual fee-paying behaviour in the context of the group can be uncomfortable. It seems a potential source of humiliation that could overwhelm other levels of interpretation. When fee-paying is discussed, the group may apparently deal with underlying resistance and feelings of deprivation and resentment, but the individuals concerned do not necessarily change their behaviour. People's habits regarding bills seem more resistant to change in a group, compared with the direct personal exchange of one-to-one psychotherapy.

Group members can use fee payment as an opportunity for individual attention outside the group. If this can be brought back into the group rather than taken at face value it can be explored and understood. The fee-paying part of the context may relate to transference issues in present and past relationships. Attempts to interact with the therapist outside of the group over fees may be attempts to recover and resolve initial transference relationships with the therapist that existed prior to entering the group. This is likely to be particularly so for group members who have experienced significant loss or had stepparents. The transition into the group can signify the death or loss of one parent and the beginning of relating to the other.

When the client fails to pay

Difficulty in paying

With a fairly substantial caseload, the chances are that one or more of the clients will have difficulty paying. Circumstances can change in unexpected ways, which leave the therapy vulnerable. Money is a very personal issue and requires the most delicate handling. Someone who is in straitened circumstances may not wish to have their therapy subsidized. The therapist can look very carefully at the family history and see what this might unwittingly repeat. Clients who have been overdominated by their mothers and never allowed to do things for themselves may need to pay for their own therapy, whatever the cost.

I have tried a number of responses, each dictated by my relationship with the client. I have charged a lower fee on the understanding that if circumstances change the difference will be made up. I have charged a lower fee on the understanding that in proportion to their available income they are paying a fee equivalent to that paid previously. I have also charged a lower fee on the firm understanding that the balance will be made up. However, the debt was limited to the amount that there was a reasonable expectation of the client repaying. Tax has to be paid on invoices issued, whether or not they are settled, and a therapist needs to avoid putting herself in a position of paying tax on money that has not been received and is unlikely to be paid.

Therapists sometimes find it necessary to stop seeing a client who cannot pay. It may be possible to point such a person in the direction of voluntary or statutory sector provision, which they might access in time. Clients who are on lower incomes can be referred to trainee therapists or encouraged to join a group, where the fees are lower. These referrals need to be made confidently by therapists who have seen the care taken by trainee therapists and so can honestly refer clients to trainees, with the confidence that they will be offered what they need. Anyone who has experience of both individual and group work can explain to clients that while therapy groups work differently from individual therapy, there are benefits to moving from individual to group. When clients are making this move they may need to consider how they can build on the work they have already done, rather than leave it behind.

The large unpaid bill

Generally the personal nature of the therapeutic relationship ensures fees are paid. It is important to hold in mind that no one wants to pay. The resistance to paying can produce useful work on withholding and expressing the hatred of the therapist. However, at some stage a therapist will have a large bill left unpaid, which cannot easily be ignored. This requires the therapist to use her anger constructively. It is easy to feel so angry that one wants nothing more to do with the client and the last thing one wants is to engage in a protracted exercise to recoup the fees. However, this leaves the therapist holding both the feelings and the debt. I have spoken to therapists who years later still feel abused and enraged by clients who could have paid but declined to do so. Harnessing the anger and pursuing the debt is one way to deal with these feelings. Of course it means admitting that we do the work for the money, and that we are dependent on the client to supply our income.

Counsellors and psychotherapists spend their lives empathizing and understanding. Supervision can sometimes be used to get a clear view of why the client is not paying and what the therapist contributes to the acting out. Is it a transference issue where the therapist has become the younger sister who must be deprived? Is it a deeper pathology – perhaps evinced by a history of defrauding others? A very clear understanding of the meaning will enable a therapist to plan a strategy to ensure the fee is paid. Where it is not open to therapeutic intervention, normal social and commercial conventions come into play.

I have spoken to people who have used the Small Claims Court and debt-collecting agencies and who report very positively on the process and the outcome. They have, of course, given the client ample chance to settle the debt. They also wrote letters saying that if the fee is not paid by a certain date they would have to put it in the hands of the debt-collection agency, or take steps to recover the bad debt through the Small Claims Court. Using a debt-collection agency is very simple and takes the matter entirely out of the therapist's hands. The agency takes a percentage of the debt for their services.

The Small Claims Court

The vast majority of claims processed through the County Court are for small sums, usually less than £1000. There may be no need to attend the court. It is possible to use an online system called Money Claim Online. The details are entered online for a registration fee, which is proportionate to the amount claimed. If the defendant either accepts liability for the debt or fails to respond to the claim, the claimant can request a judgement online without setting foot in the courtroom. Rather than describe all the detail here, which in any case will change from time to time, I refer the reader to a description of how to use the Small Claims Court, available at www.courtservice. gov.uk; or you can log on directly to www.moneyclaim.gov.uk. A support line answering questions is available on 0845 6015935.

It is advisable to research whether the debtor is worth suing and able to pay up. The User Guide at www.courtservice.gov.uk has details of the Registry Trust, which will know if there have been previous claims against the debtor, and the Insolvency Service, which records if the person is bankrupt or if their company is in liquidation, in which case there may be little chance of recouping the debt. The fee for lodging your claim is relatively small and if you win you can recover your costs. A typical psychotherapist's claim for unpaid fees should be difficult to contest; however, if you were to lose, your ex-client would be able to claim expenses and court fees.

One colleague reported a difficulty with the Small Claims Court some years ago. Even when he had a judgement, the client still did not pay, which meant bailiffs had to be called in, requiring an upfront fee from the therapist. However, if the defendant has a job, an 'attachment of earnings order' can be applied for, which tells the defendant's employer to deduct the money from the defendant's earnings and pay it to the therapist. This is not possible with the self-employed. If the debtor has savings a third-party debt order would freeze the defendant's bank account and pay directly. Further details are available in the Consumers' Association's *Which?* report 'A guide to using the Small Claims Court' (*Which?*, 2003) and on www.courtservice.gov.uk.

Managing the finances

The bank account controls the business. Keep control of the bank account and you keep control of your business. Tax is straightforward and with good advice can be kept to a minimum. Properly charged expenses are preferable to any clever scams, particularly when they fail. Integrity is a vital part of the relationship with clients. When clients ask whether I would prefer cash, I am always interested to try to understand what it tells me about them or their expectations of me. It is unwise for a therapist to be tempted to delude herself about the need to be scrupulous about tax. Early on in my career a colleague was reported to the Inland Revenue by one of her more disturbed clients. She had to endure a full and completely unwarranted investigation of her finances. Therapists are in the business of dealing with negative transference, and attacks on the therapist can be quite enough to deal with, without feeling the full might of Her Majesty's Inspector of Taxes being brought to bear. In more usual circumstances the Inland Revenue are extremely helpful and are there to explain the tax legislation that exists. Therapists have had to pay VAT since 1994. VAT is only payable once earnings have risen above the VAT limit (£56,000 in 2003; further information www.hmce.gov.uk). However, one needs to note it is a tax on turnover, not profit, i.e. VAT is payable on gross income.

An accountant or the local tax office will know what expenditure a therapist can reasonably claim against tax. I claim expenses associated with renting consulting rooms, use of home as an office, training costs, accountancy fees, books and conferences, travel, stationery, postage, telephone, office equipment, supervision and flowers. It is necessary to have receipts to match the expenses. If the person who cleans the consulting room does not provide a receipt the cost will not be tax allowable. If I stay away from home, working, the expenses I claim are those I incur. It is better to remember everything spent than to inflate claims. Nowadays a claim for a firstclass fare means travelling first class and keeping the receipt.

It is easy to overlook small receipts, forgetting to ask the taxi for one and walking out of the stationers with the new file but without the receipt. Working away from home on training events, I will eat in restaurants and am now hyper-alert to remembering the receipt, having discovered a direct inverse relationship between the quality of the food, and perhaps the quantity of the wine consumed, and my ability to remember to take a copy of the bill away with me. Safeguarding the receipt is another challenge. A colleague has a frog to help him. The frog, a giant bulldog clip, sits on the mantelpiece and any receipt entering the house is immediately fed to the frog, which guards it until the termly reckoning. For trips away, which accumulate significant expenses, I try to sit on the train home and list what I have spent. I write on the outside of an envelope and put the receipts I have collected inside it.

Keeping track of when clients pay

I have tried various systems to keep track of payments. I have kept a log of fee notes issued and paid. I have kept a card with me, which records all payments, and I have kept individual accounts. None is perfect but what I value is simplicity and accessibility. If I have to throw my family off the computer before I can record the information, it will not get done. I will be tempted to keep multiple lists, none of which will be complete. Modern electronic diaries allow the amounts to be entered directly into a spreadsheet, which can then be copied to the main accounts on a computer. If the names of the clients are to be kept confidential a cross-referencing system may need to be set up.

Before the advent of electronic diaries I kept a card in my wallet where I could tick or enter when people paid (Figure 4.1). This scored high on reliability because I always had the card on me and I could access it instantly. Of course I needed the payments entered elsewhere as well, in

Name	Jane	Mary	John	Helen	Arthur
Fee					
January					
February					
March					

Figure 4.1 **Client payments**

case my wallet was stolen. If clients paid the same each month it just needed a tick. If it was different each month I could enter the amount. When I was conducting a group the card would be just for that group.

One nightmare is the cheque that has disappeared down the back of the couch. If I am thinking of confronting a client who has not paid or if I am preparing to interpret his resistance, I need to be sure his cheque has not been swept up with my junk mail. With a small practice, memory may serve to remind me who has paid, but with a good-sized practice, systems are essential. Computer programs like Excel will extract an account for an individual in the event of any misunderstanding.

Preparing the accounts

Keeping track of income and expenditure only means writing it down. Whatever system is used for recording, it needs both to suit the person doing it and to be convenient. Perhaps the first decision is whether to do manual or computer entries. It is difficult to escape computers completely and the final accounts at the end of the year will have to be typed up. However, manual entries are perfectly good for the day-to-day operation. The great advantage of learning to use Excel, the Microsoft spreadsheet, is that it will do all the adding up accurately. Anyone who becomes familiar with Excel can of course use it to analyse which work is financially rewarding and which is less so.

Cheques can be paid into a practice account and then recorded in a cashbook. Some banks will agree to cheques being paid in by post. I record the date of the cheque and its number, as well as what it is for. This forms a long list. The record in my bank paying-in book, which shows the name and the amount paid in on a certain date, has been useful where I suspect a discrepancy has crept into my accounts.

Cashbook

A typical cashbook would have entries as shown in Figure 4.2.

A record of what is paid in and out should reveal how much is in the account and the state of the cash flow. Cash flow can be the bane of a small business and it may be necessary to loan oneself money rather than risk going overdrawn. Alternatively a relatively inexpensive overdraft facility can be set up on a business account.

Date	Fees	Cheque no.	Training expenses	Stationery, telephone and books	Travel	Room hire	Prof. memb. fees	Prof. expenses, accounts, etc.	Total income	Total expend.	Bank balance

Figure 4.2 **Cashbook**

Chapter 5
Marketing your skills

Our potential clients need help with taking the first step. Someone looking for sources of insight and help is spoilt for choice. It is our responsibility to articulate what therapy offers and how clients will benefit. A good salesperson is one who gives the buyer the confidence to find and purchase what he needs. Experienced therapists who feel that self-promotion is not for them might learn something from the old-established family firms who took the same line and then struggled in a competitive commercial market.

Overcoming inhibitions about marketing

There are plenty of people out there vaguely looking for therapy. They are easily deterred by not knowing how to find someone or who to trust. Promoting ourselves can feel pushy but we need to see it as part of meeting our potential clients' need. Prospective clients do not always understand about therapy and frequently think that their problems are not sufficiently serious to bother anyone else, or to waste a counsellor's time. It is very British to struggle on, telling oneself that there are others who are worse off and that one should be grateful for small mercies. Money can also be a deterrent. Clients either feel a social failure if they have to pay for it, or cannot bring themselves to spend the necessary money on themselves. I think we have a role in helping people deal with these issues.

In this context, marketing means educating people and providing the information they need. It also means explaining who you are, how you can help and how you are relevant to their lives. Society, newspaper headlines and magazine articles influence how clients present their problems. They are more likely to feel that you can meet their need if you are using the same language. Everyone knows counselling helps with depression. Where the depression is masked by other distress, counsellors have to demonstrate that they have something particular that will meet the need and deal with the distress. In my practice people are increasingly complaining of sleep disorder.

Knowing what issues are facing the clients you want to help can focus your appeal to them. You need to know the particular characteristics of the people you want to communicate with. If you want to fill your daytime spaces you will need to identify people who have that flexibility. Whereas if you have particular expertise with parenting issues or alcohol you will need to think about how these people can be contacted. When approaching a workplace you might want to talk about relieving stress, resolving interpersonal conflict, reducing performance anxiety, and containing worries about the future. These are issues facing personnel at different stages of their career within the same company. Framing it positively and focusing on offering a solution rather than drawing attention to the problem seems to make it easier for people to respond.

Depressive anxiety

Therapists can be overwhelmed by depressive anxiety about their practice at any stage in their career. What is difficult is to find a place where this can be explored openly. Part of the task of qualifying as a therapist is to lay claim to the identity of therapist and make it your own. A therapist is particularly vulnerable to professional depressive anxiety during the period following qualification, having left behind the old identity but not yet having fully developed the muscles of the new professional self. Therapists who have years of experience may suffer similar insecurities. Someone who decides to make a major change, such as a move from a secure setting like 'Relate' into private practice, may suffer some of the same uncertainty. Still others may be suffering a mid-life crisis, looking to colleagues for the enthusiasm to keep working creatively.

The established therapist's dilemma

Established therapists have a particular problem. At some stage their practice is full and they decline to take new referrals. Referrers accommodate and refer elsewhere. Some time later three or four clients all finish their excellent therapy at the same time and the therapist is left with a depleted practice and no referrals coming in. They are probably out of practice at having to market themselves and feel they should not have to, at this stage in their career. Maybe colleagues who used to refer to them have retired. It is easy to be reminded of some of the highly esteemed old family firms that have gone to the wall because they took the attitude 'We are not the sort of company that needs to advertise, our reputation goes before us'. Senior psychotherapists are running a business, and even the most prestigious businesses work hard to keep up their profile in the wider world. Established psychotherapists have to bite the bullet, and decide which is the least painful way to alert a new group of people to the fact that they are open to referrals.

Recognizing the competition

Therapists are in competition with one another for clients but rarely talk about it. We prefer to see ourselves as esteemed colleagues who refer to each other to the mutual benefit of our clients and ourselves. This allows some pervasively destructive forces to be denied and go underground. Established therapists can be helpful and encouraging to newly qualified colleagues. However, a closer examination will sometimes reveal that alongside the referral there is an unspoken obligation. The younger therapists are reassured, encouraged and coaxed into behaving in ways that will not threaten to change the status quo.

Forming referral networks

Where the competitive instincts can be harnessed, it is sometimes easier to resist depressive anxiety if one has supportive colleagues. A peer supervision group is one answer, particularly if part of its remit is helping to promote one another's practice. If I don't have any evening vacancies maybe my peer group colleague does. I can help the referrer to refer confidently because I know something of my colleague's work through supervision. It is often easier to sing the praises of a colleague one has genuine confidence in, than it is to put oneself forward. This kind of setting is particularly useful where the practitioner is doing something complex like running analytic groups. If four colleagues each have three clients waiting to start a group, it might be better to pool resources and get two groups started. If these are successful the interest generated will make it easier for two more groups to be started so everyone has what they need. However, this requires a level of good faith between the practitioners, which is more likely to emerge if the project is taken on with serious good intention and planning.

The conflict between co-operation and competition is a constant tension and probably accounts for the depressive anxiety that overwhelms groups that are set up to support the efforts of psychotherapists in private practice. I can recommend two models that have worked for me.

The Clinical Section model

When I qualified I was fortunate in meeting a group of people who were interested in thinking about the institutional, cultural, personal and practical dynamics that contributed to the pressures psychotherapists work under. We met on Saturday mornings once a month to exchange experience and think about the realities of conducting a private practice. Importantly the meetings were open to the whole institute and we escaped the usual dynamic where the anxiety and criticism located in the newly qualified members and ignored. In bringing together a number of thoughtful, innovative people we were able to learn from one another in very practical ways. Much of the impetus for this book comes from those initial meetings. What was important was that we had started with a difficulty, which we wanted to understand. Only once we understood some of the unconscious and institutional dynamics did we start to think about what we could do to address them.

We were able to debunk a number of myths. It had been easy to imagine that people with other trainings struggled less than we did, or that other colleagues were effortlessly successful. One of the more interesting dilemmas was whether the constrained behaviour traditionally associated with a respected therapist was essential or was in fact a cause of our difficulties. Many psychotherapeutic traditions evolved from psychoanalysis and medicine, so we tended not to advertise. It has been difficult to question these assumptions.

Training institutes are membership bodies, and this was an example of members getting together and working out what they needed from an institute rather than passively hoping that the institute would know what they needed and provide it for them. The creativity could easily have been lost as the meetings gradually petered out. However, it had become clear that one factor that inhibited us from developing successful practices was the lack of free flow of information. The confidentiality associated with our work had somehow contaminated our thinking processes. There may well have been fears of shame and envy from those with more or less successful practices. However, if we did not know what each of us had to offer, how could we refer to each other and encourage others to do the same?

Petrol stations and shoe shops

Of course we were all afraid we would lose more than we would gain. However, a friend, who explained about shoe shops and petrol stations, helped me. If you want to buy a pair of shoes you go to the town with the most shoe shops. If you want to start up a shoe shop business the best place to be is next door to another shoe shop. Shell and Texaco build their garages on the opposite sides of the same junction because it is going to increase custom. Thus although all my instincts told me to be isolationist, it did ring true that the more good, successful psychotherapists there were around, the more people would go for psychotherapy and the easier my practice would be.

A Clinical Section of the institute was created to promote the clinical work of the membership. It was intended as a flexible structure, which would accommodate whatever initiative the membership could work on together to promote psychotherapy in general as well as individual practitioners. The dialogue shifted to an annual large group discussion and then to individuals and projects. A referral network was set up. The medical model was resisted and everyone involved in the referral system was invited to take part in assessing people looking for therapy. With a rota system and an answerphone the referral system has gone from strength to strength.

Participants received the occasional referral through the network but also put themselves on the map in people's minds as the person to contact if you are looking for something in, for example, South or Central London. Equally important, it allowed participants to place referrals they could not take on at that time. Therapists knew what colleagues were doing and who to refer to. GPs and others who send people to us for therapy want us to take them on personally, but failing that they want their client sent somewhere they can feel good about. The last thing they want is the person back in their lap, looking expectant.

Professional help was brought in to redesign our literature so that the information about the institute's referral network reflected how we saw ourselves. Fiona Macintosh worked for Artloud, producing marketing packages for organizations like Save the Children. She was also an art therapist so we were confident she would understand what we wanted to say and the sensitivities of both therapists and potential clients. What was designed was simple, stylish and something anyone would be pleased to be associated with. Other creative designers followed. There is a tendency for psychotherapists to produce drab, wordy literature, which reinforces the distaste potential clients have for therapy.

The Psychotherapy Referral Service

Each school of psychotherapy or counselling jealously guards its own principles and ideas and it is easy to become inward-looking, missing out on developments happening elsewhere in the professional world. I joined a referral network made up of therapists who had done a variety of different trainings. We shared a common commitment to the kind of ideals embodied by the Women's Therapy Centre. A core group of members met bimonthly to promote the group and review how the referrals were going. All members met twice a year to share food and thoughts. It has been invaluable having colleagues involved in different training institutes, because we have been able to pool the knowledge of each group of people, learn from their experience and pick up on good ideas at an early stage. The network was called the Psychotherapy Referral Service, South and West (London). Collaborating together, to minimize the cost and the effort, we were able to have a website, www.psychotherapyservice.com, advertise in Yellow Pages and put leaflets in libraries, etc. The referral service operated very simply as an answerphone in someone's cupboard under the stairs. Turns were taken to access the machine remotely and answer the calls. The success of the group was down to respecting and liking one another. Care was taken over who could join. It meant that we could place clients confidently with whichever therapist best suited, either in terms of geography or approach.

Networking at training events

Therapists like to refer to colleagues they have met. Training events and conferences are traditional forms of networking, which involve people beyond the therapist's immediate circle. Such events provide the opportunity to work together with other therapists and to share particular expertise. If I have felt comfortable, or inspired, talking with someone in a workshop I will bear him or her in mind when making referrals. A therapist can spend her life going to meetings, and discrimination is called for. Training institutes and membership organizations provide the opportunity for continuing professional development, as do sections of the British Association for Counselling and Psychotherapy (BACP), British Confederation of Psychotherapists (BCP) and UK Council for Psychotherapy (UKCP). Planning creatively will pay off and help the therapist to focus on the most relevant aspects at any given time, whether they are clinical, supervisory, writing, time management, marketing, or physical well-being.

Teaching, cards and websites

Teaching and doing talks are good ways of letting people know who you are. For more information see the section on teaching in Chapter 8. Members of the audience develop a sense of whether they would like to work with you and whether they would trust you with their referrals. Before doing the lecture it is worth thinking about which aspects of your practice you might want this audience to be aware of. Inevitably I am so preoccupied with doing the lecture that I forget to mention that I run a 'group for professional therapists' or whatever it is that I think might interest them. However, I am now the proud owner of a business card. The local printers produced it cheaply and quickly. I no longer scribble my telephone number on the back of an envelope when someone would like to keep in contact with me at the end of a talk. The card encourages people to check out my website (www.groupanalyst.com) where they can find for themselves whatever I failed to mention. People can take their time, anonymously, to check out who I am and what I do.

Designing a website

Creating websites is getting easier all the time and can be very simple. A simple website can cost about £100 for a web hosting package that you design yourself plus the domain name for £50. Finding a domain name could not be simpler. Log on to the provider, type in the domain name you would like to have and they will say instantly if it is available. There are various types of domain name; for example .co.uk indicates a UK business, .com indicates USA or international, and .org indicates an organization or society. The referral network I belong to, www.psychotherapyservice.com, went for something more sophisticated and employed a designer who manages the site. Keeping a website up to date is no small task but it is essential. A notice board covered with out-of-date notices is bad enough. A neglected website conveys a very unfortunate message about the care the therapist will take with the client.

If you are going to bring someone in to design the site you will save money if you can be clear about the following points.

- What you are offering.
- What your unique selling point is.
- Who your potential clients are.
- Why people want to come to you.
- What your key concepts are.
- What the purpose of the site is.
- What you know about your market.

You will probably need 10–15 pages. Any artwork, logos, graphics and text you can provide will reduce the cost and ensure you feel comfortable with the result. People find websites through directories and through links from other sites. I put a talk on Projective Identification on the Group Analytic Practice website (www.gapractice.org.uk). This was picked up by a website based in Israel and from there references to it appeared on US and UK websites. Anyone wanting to read it came to my website and probably looked at what else I was doing. Links can be a reciprocal arrangement or a way of providing more information. Most people come to the website from directories and search engines. The BACP has an excellent online directory (www.counselling.co.uk). Commercial directories and search engines, e.g. yell.com and google.com, will invite registration sometimes for a fee. Instructions on how to register are on the home web page of the directory.

Promoting your therapy service

In this section Fiona Macintosh, an art therapist who recently relocated her practice to Scotland, and Jackie Reiter, a counsellor who set up her own practice (One to One Counselling), describe their particular approaches to marketing and publicity.

Fiona Macintosh

Selling yourself is a hard thing to do. It does not sit well with the therapy professionals, trained as they are to be attentive to others' needs. I came into the art psychotherapy profession in 1990. Alongside this I did graphic design and graphics/media training for small non-governmental organizations and international workers' federations, to help them to get their message across in design, theatre, radio and TV. I found these skills useful to building up my art therapy sessional work in Scotland, particularly in thinking about how best to approach and tailor my message to potential employers.

I soon found out, in Scotland, that art therapy was generally perceived of as another form of occupational therapy or something artists could provide. Within such a climate my profession's association was a support. However, I still had to find the work. I started scanning newspapers but advertisements for art therapists do not exist. Instead I took note of local charities and organizations working with ex-offenders, the homeless, drug users, prostitution, areas within mental health, and children-at-risk programmes. I used the telephone directory to contact local organizations; schools' special needs departments, hospitals and prisons.

Sometimes, when I didn't know whom I needed to speak to, the receptionist in frustration plugged me into the personnel department, rarely a good idea. Persistence, warmth and humour usually got me back on track to finding the relevant person. Once found, I would briefly explain my work and how this could back up their work/project. The outcome so far is sessional work with some charities, the local school, a nearby day centre and an NHS multidisciplinary mental health team.

Based on my experience the following might be a useful checklist.

1. *Do you want to be self-employed or employed?* Do you have any choice given the job market?

2. *Where do you want to work?* Within a psychotherapeutic environment? In health, education or the private charitable world?

3. *Who is your potential client group?* The general public, elderly, homeless, ethnic minorities, refugees, special needs children? What other information do you need to know about this group, i.e. age, ethnicity, gender, and educational level?

4. *Where do you access these people?* Through interface organizations, i.e. doctors' surgeries, hospitals, special needs schools, nurseries to access parents, youth clubs, old age pensioner clubs, charities supporting people with special needs?

5. *How do you access these people?* You need to know:
   • What are the main issues the client group seeks to resolve?
   • Does the interface organization do this?
   • What is the work being done by the interface professionals?
   • Do the professionals have understanding of your profession?
   • How can you present your professional skills to dovetail and strengthen the interface organization's work with its clients?

Armed with information on the above you need to do the following:

• Find out who is the key contact: get it right first time. Find out who will be the person likely to be interested in your work, and also able to open doors within their organization: GPs, head of special needs, nursery nurse, youth worker, club manager, charity project managers.

• Send them a tailored letter outlining in brief what you can offer their clients.

• End with a request to meet.

• Once this has been sent or emailed, call a week later to ask if they would like to meet.

• At the same time request if you could visit their programme/project/centre because you are interested to understand their work better.

- Meet this person and/or their team, i.e. social workers/psychiatric team, etc.
- Offer your service to them based on prior knowledge of what they do.
- Leave the professionals with a very brief and succinct outline letter or leaflet on what your practice can achieve, with contact details and fees. Hand out your card.
- They may want to discuss using your service amongst themselves.
- Ask when they will contact you on their decision.

Publicity

You may be able to do this for yourself on your computer, though I have yet to know a psychotherapist who can produce well-designed publicity, and a poor image will do you no favours. Invest in your image. It does not need to be expensive. A one-colour leaflet on good quality paper with a clean, calm, typographically smart design will provide reassurance and confidence in you. A website is useful to give credibility, though it is rarely a means through which to gain work on its own.

Your publicity benefits from a consistent style. Look at what kind of publicity your peers use. Is it effectively worded and attractively geared towards the intended audience? Work with a designer whose work you know is effective, maybe because a colleague has recommended them, or a designer who will sympathize with what you do. Discuss what publicity you need with the designer. You might want a leaflet laser-printed, or you may need a bigger print run. It is helpful to have quotes in writing once you have agreed on paper quality, quantity of colours and print run.

- Be persistent.
- It is essential to keep a record of your follow-up contacting, to stay on track.
- Time your follow-up calls to appear professionally responsible but not over-eager.
- Pace yourself to remain optimistic. The tone of your voice and your clarity, self-assurance and sincerity can make or break a new contact.

Jackie Reiter

Having worked with various different communication media throughout my professional life, as a newly qualified counsellor I realized the importance of a strong and attractive image if I was to market myself successfully in an extremely competitive environment. North London is second only to California in terms of the ratio of therapists to the general population. I decided to produce a leaflet, which I would use to approach my target audience – GPs, employment assistance programmes and the general public. I had identified a leafleting company, which would place my leaflets in appropriate venues: libraries, community centres, gyms, arts centres, etc.

What did I want the leaflet to convey?

- About my work: that I am a professional, effective and approachable counsellor. I decided to give my practice a name - One to One Counselling. This name accomplishes two important things: it indicates the way I work and implies that the practice has an identity which goes beyond one individual. I think this inspires confidence.

- About me: I gave biographical details to give a fuller sense of who I am and what my life experience has been, which I believe enhances my credibility as a counsellor. This proved effective as several people who contacted me mentioned being attracted by some element of my personal experience.

- My telephone number and email address.

Refining the text

I spent time refining the text because I wanted it to be straightforward – not to get into laborious definitions of counselling – and to convey a sense of my individual approach and style. At the same time I wanted it to look clean and smart and not overloaded with text. At this point I approached a graphic designer whose work I knew and respected, and she produced a design which formed the basis for further refinement in order to create an effective logo that would say something about the counselling process.

I then had feedback from the leaflet distributor who argued for amendments to the design, taking into account the way the leaflet would be displayed on the stands. At first I resisted this because I was so attached to the design as it stood, but in the end I agreed and am glad that I did, because this form of displaying the leaflet has proved highly effective, producing several clients.

Chapter 6
Time management

For therapists, time both stands still and rushes past. The practitioner who emerges from the timeless world of the unconscious is faced with the dynamic administration tasks, which will expand to fill the space available to them. How we manage our time and ourselves will influence whether we enjoy the job or are persecuted by the non-clinical aspects.

Conceptualizing time

Psychotherapists have a particular relationship with time. We create a place for our clients where time stands still. Angela Molnos (1995) describes this as the lure of timelessness. We create the illusion that we have all the time in the world, and that we have nothing else to do or think about. Small children experience time as starting in the morning, ending in the evening and starting all over again the next day. I think we recreate this experience in the consulting room for 50 minutes. Of course at the end of the session we return to the terror of time's arrow and the idea that time marches on. Time that has passed is lost for ever. This linear concept of time carries with it the inevitability of our own mortality. We are currently living through an unprecedented acceleration of linear time, which alters our experience of time and space. 'Not only has the world shrunk, but also time itself seems to get shattered and fragmented at every step. Life is governed by time-schedules. We have become increasingly time-conscious, time obsessed. We worry more about time itself than we do about what we actually do' (Molnos, 1995: 8).

Managing the paperwork

So how do therapists straddle these two worlds? Faced with an in-tray piled so high it is likely to topple over, it would be wonderful to disappear into a timeless 50 minutes no longer exposed to the pressures of time-consuming tasks. Time management books recommend getting organized, tackling jobs as they come in and learning to say 'no' to unimportant tasks. However, issues of freedom and control immediately arise. Therapists spend all week with their time rigidly allocated to whoever needs it. The idea that the rest of the time should be similarly organized, in the service of efficiency, could lead to despair. It is not acceptable to neglect the clients but ignoring the administration can come quite easily. Feeling persecuted by paperwork or thwarted by answerphones can be useful outlets for the feelings a therapist cannot allow herself to have about clients. Ved Varma (1997) in his book *Stress in Psychotherapists* describes the pressures experienced by psychotherapists and examines how the effects vary according to the problems they treat, the settings in which they work and their professional and personal development. At times the therapist might envy the clients. Faced with a pile of filing, or accounts that will not add up, it is easy to long for the kind of support we give our clients. It seems unlikely to be forthcoming and in the meantime we may have to learn something from time management ideas.

Distant elephants

Of course it is not really about managing time: it is about managing ourselves. I have to reconcile myself to doing some of what the time management people suggest if I am to have any time to myself. One thing that definitely works is standing over the bin whilst opening the post. Suddenly it is less effort to throw a letter away than to add it to the pile. It is not easy to get a realistic perspective on what we can and cannot manage. Butler and Hope (1997), who publish an excellent brief chapter on time management, talk about 'distant elephants'. Large specimens seem to regularly slip unnoticed into my life. When asked to run a workshop in a year's time it is easy to say 'yes'. At that distance it seems quite a manageable undertaking. It is only when it gets nearer that it becomes clear quite how much time and energy it will require. 'Distant elephants' are to be identified and avoided wherever possible. Similarly it is helpful to realize that saying 'yes' to one thing is saying 'no' to something else. It is no longer a question of whether I want to do something but rather whether I would give up something else to do it.

Once past the desk

I have completely failed at the 'once past the desk' manoeuvre. This is where a tricky letter takes up residence in the in-tray and although it is read and thought about a number of times, 'now' never seems quite the right moment to tackle it. A 'once past the desk' rule means the second time it is read it has to be dealt with. Failing that a time is put aside when it will be attended to and it is done in the allotted time. Of course the temptation is simply to stop looking in the in-tray because whatever is there will have to be dealt with. I prefer the sound of the 'Banjo' approach – Bang A Nasty Job Off (Black, 1987). This means deciding at the beginning of the day which is the most unpleasant task on the 'to do' list and simply doing it. It is unlikely to be as bad as anticipated, which gets the day off to a good start.

Using routine to provide structure

Getting started is half the problem. Generally we don't have bosses standing over us and we have to be self-motivating. It is amazing how the morning can disappear on the back of a cup of coffee and the newspaper. Building in a routine that works and does not feel persecutory is probably a good idea. Efficient colleagues report that they add half an hour for administration at the end of the morning or set one morning a month aside in the diary to do the accounts. That way it just happens.

Managing ourselves

Life is so short it demands that we spend our time on the things we value. This means identifying how we want to earn a living and planning how to achieve it. If someone else's ideas are leading the way, are they moving in the appropriate direction? Much of the anger and resentment in relationships between therapists comes from individuals who have not dared to set their own agenda. They have substituted a role of helping others with their projects, and then feel used, frustrated and unrewarded. Writing goals down or doing a paper exercise will reveal realistic ideas and what is important to you. It is not just about what you want to do but also about who you want to be. Time managers suggest thinking about where you want to be in five years' time or what you would like people to be thinking about you in five years' time. There is an example of setting goals in the chapter on 'Practice development' (Chapter 3). However, it is also important to look at what gives you satisfaction and what you need in order to grow as a person. Then in making a decision you can act in accordance with the values and goals outlined. These values and goals can help plan continuing professional development so that you meet your needs and do not just follow everyone else in whatever is fashionable.

Saying 'no'

Saying 'no' is an essential skill. Assertiveness training helps but it comes down to being logical and unemotional, but firm. We can usually say 'no' when it really matters but much of the time we are happy for the needs of others to rule what we do. It doesn't seem worth the effort required to say 'no' and cause others difficulty. We only live once and it is probably better to learn to say 'no' earlier rather than later. How often we say 'no' is a measure of how available we are to colleagues and clients. Someone who is always available has a warm glow but probably doesn't achieve what they would like to. Shutting a door or turning on an answerphone can give a clear indication of whether a distraction would be welcome or not. No one would interrupt a client session but actually I need to concentrate just as hard on some of the administration if I am going to get it finished. Interruptions steal time.

Pareto's Law

Much as we might like to steal time from somewhere or live on borrowed time, the reality is that we can only make the best of the time we have. There is a limit to how many hours a week we can work so at some point we have to actively manage ourselves. Pareto's Law says that 20% of time at work is spent doing things that account for 80% of results and 80% of the time is spent doing things that account for only 20% of the results. The effective 20% is made up of tasks like planning, setting up systems, learning and building relationships. Dealing with a crisis gets the adrenaline going and is very exciting, but setting up systems to prevent a crisis is more cost-effective, if rather boring. Fire fighting is exciting, fire prevention is dull. Buying a personal organizer and taking the time to set the systems up is probably time well invested if it means everything is in one place and can easily be found.

A 'To do' list can distinguish what is important from what is urgent. It is difficult to give up the reactive position of doing whatever is most pressing rather than what will get on top of the work. Making a new list each day and putting the most important job at the top is probably the best way forward. However, it is possible to confuse making the list with having done the job, or to fall for the lure of the comfortable task and do an unimportant task that can easily be done, while avoiding the one that is rather more necessary.

Starters and finishers

The world can be thought of in terms of starters and finishers. Finishers would not dream of starting a new project until the present one is off their hands. The pleasure is not so much in doing the work as in completing it. They seem to be able to keep moving the project forward rather then extracting every ounce of meaning from the process. Finishing something gives a sense of achievement and fulfilment. Starters on the other hand have a desk strewn with possible projects and good ideas as well as work in progress. A starter will enjoy setting about numerous interesting projects but life would be much easier if the mindset of a finisher could be cultivated alongside.

Taking on other people's work

In clinical work I resist taking on my clients' projections. However, with colleagues it can be a different matter entirely. If someone behaves as if I could do a task better than them or as if they cannot manage without my help, I fall for it instantly and offer to do it for them. If I know how the photocopier works it makes sense for me to show them, even if I should be making some telephone calls. Of course it would be better if I resisted the flattering projection of competence, pointed out their competence and encouraged them to do the work rather than adding to my workload. Other times I might find myself accepting a responsibility that rightly belongs elsewhere. Projections have to fit with the recipient and each of us is likely to be vulnerable to different approaches. Clarity, about who is responsible for what, helps people negotiate tasks sensibly.

Perfectionism

Those of us who have a perfectionist streak will usually deny the label. We do not recognize it because we never succeed in being perfect and more readily see ourselves as inefficient and hopeless. It is difficult to know when standards are being set unnecessarily high. If every job is done with the same care and attention we give our clients it gives an illusion of safety and protection from criticism. It is difficult to trust that it will be supportable for us to give less than our best to the particular job in front of us. However, it is not possible to do everything well, and discriminating the vital work from the pressing and demanding will create space.

Procrastination is the thief of time

Procrastination is letting low priority tasks get in the way of high priority ones, and it is rife. When I signed on for a research degree the university took procrastination so seriously that the first lecture was on how to deal with it. They outlined all the usual suspects that might stop us writing:

- I ought to tidy my desk/the house first.
- I cannot throw the children off the computer.
- I don't quite feel up to it today, I'll do better tomorrow.
- I have got to make that urgent telephone call.

- I'll just have a cup of coffee first.
- There is plenty of time.
- It is OK to indulge myself; I'll get down to it tomorrow.
- I need to think about it a bit more.

At the time, these thoughts seem convincing, but clearly they are allowing us to avoid something we fear. The solution seems to be not to fight the feeling but instead just to do something. The initial inertia will be overcome by something as simple as rereading what was written yesterday or making some rough notes. Once the barrier to starting is passed, it is easier to keep going. Breaking jobs down into manageable chunks is always a good idea.

Procrastination can be linked to fear of making the wrong decision or needing a high level of certainty and thinking through every option before making the decision. Of course this is exhausting and places a heavy load on the memory. It is not surprising if it becomes tempting to try and pass the decision on to someone else. It is difficult to change this mindset but inroads can be made by deliberately taking responsibility for a decision or thinking about the worst that would happen if the decision, turns out badly. I think it is particularly difficult for therapists because our referrals depend on our standing with our clients and colleagues, who can be quite censorious. It is worth finding out how other people make decisions and employing the kind of time limit that they would use.

Rewarding ourselves

Perhaps the most important time management activity is noticing what has been achieved and areas that have been managed well. If starting to implement time management is pleasurable, it is likely to be repeated until it becomes a good habit and eventually comes naturally.

Section 3

Diversifying as a therapist

Working in different settings

Working in a GP surgery
The voluntary sector
Working alongside other professionals
Mentoring
Beyond the consulting room

Portfolio person, teacher and supervisor

Teaching
Supervision
The supervision setting

Chapter 7
Working in different settings

Working in contrasting settings with colleagues is rewarding and challenging. Understanding the culture of the National Health Service, the voluntary sector and the world of mentoring will make it easier for therapists to transfer their skills from one situation to another and to manage therapy where more than one professional is involved.

Therapists working in private practice can easily become isolated and lose touch with the rest of the working world. Loneliness and lack of career development start to become a problem. Working part-time in the NHS or the voluntary sector, where the therapist has the advantage of a multidisciplinary team, is a stimulating solution. Colleagues encountered there are likely to be conversant with current good working practice in equal opportunities, professional responsibilities and new technology. Independent therapists do their best to stay up to date but this is more easily achieved in a setting where training courses are routinely available. The fees earned may not be high but the hidden benefits more than make up for this. While the counselling skills are eminently transferable the approach to the work is quite distinctive. Understanding the values that underlie the different settings will make for a smoother transition.

Mentoring requires a step further. This will particularly suit those with experience of the business world. However, there is considerable scope for mentoring within the voluntary, health and social services sectors. Therapists have been moving right outside the consulting room and applying their skills in the commercial sector acting as organizational consultants or conducting staff groups. This chapter describes the experience of therapists in these different settings.

Working in a GP surgery

In recent years many therapists have been employed in general practitioner (GP) surgeries. In general this transition has been well thought out and appropriately instituted. It is, however, a very particular environment to work in. The therapist will be working in a medical team, which will be multidisciplinary. The work will suit a therapist who enjoys engaging with a variety of people with different viewpoints. The other professionals will be coming at issues from a different perspective and inevitably they will not see it the same way that the therapist does. A therapist who fails to understand this could feel isolated, lacking people who share her perception of events. It is useful to have worked in a hospital or to have gained psychiatric experience from working in a department of psychiatry. Therapists without psychiatric backgrounds might need to ensure they become familiar with the language, structures and practices employed in the primary care trusts, to make sense of the cultural context. Wilke and Freeman (2001) give a clear description of the changes that have taken place in primary care provision in recent years and the demands placed on those working in that context.

In this setting it is likely that the clients will not be starting from a psychological perspective. Working in a medical setting gives the therapist an awareness of how the psychological and physical interrelate. The therapist will need to give credence to the physical. Patients come in with both physical and psychological elements to their story but their focus will be to a large extent on the physical. Both the therapist and the doctor may be thinking in psychological terms but that is not usually where the patient is starting. The patient will be concerned about their physical symptoms. While some GP practices encourage psychological awareness amongst their patients it is probably a mistake to anticipate this to be at a high level. People are accessing a medical system because they think they are medically ill.

The patient is a GP practice patient and this means that confidentiality operates slightly differently. The therapist is not working alone and cannot hold the confidentiality independently. It may need to be shared with the team. This does not mean revealing the details of the conversations but being prepared to share how the treatment is going, otherwise the therapist will not get the back-up of her colleagues. The workplace ethos is one of relying on one another. The therapist cannot afford to be prissy or holier than thou about confidentiality and has to reach a professional understanding with colleagues. The therapist may only be in the GP surgery once a week; others are there more of the time and the patient will be going back to see them. In an emergency it is the full-time colleagues who will step in and deal with any difficulty.

Taking the trouble to educate colleagues about how therapy works will help to build up relationships that operate with trust on both sides. The therapist has a role to explain clearly who can be helped by therapy so that appropriate people can be referred. If others working in the GP practice truly understand what the therapist needs from the practice in order to function efficiently, they are more likely to provide it. GPs will want to work together with the therapist to learn how they can get the best from her. It is difficult to meet and talk in a busy practice where there is little time, but people do listen when they are interested and feel someone has something to say. It is important to have the confidence and the authority to offer a professional opinion. A therapist who is clear in her own mind what she wants to say is more likely to deliver it in a way that is taken notice of. This builds a relationship with colleagues which is respected. A therapist in primary care will probably always be, or feel, marginal. The therapeutic culture will not prevail but if it is perceived as helpful and flexible it might become a valued alternative to what the GP is offering.

The number of sessions is usually limited and it will be difficult to practise classical therapy. Many therapists report the challenge they face in adapting their style and learning about short-term focused work. However, they also convey a sense of having learnt something important and helpful which has significantly extended their repertoire. A high level of skill and experience is required to do short-term work well (Molnos, 1995). The frustration of having a limited number of sessions is somewhat balanced by the sheer number of people who can be given the opportunity to reflect on their lives. Where patients can be referred on or where there is other provision, such as an analytic group, some sessions may become akin to a protracted assessment. The aim then is to ensure that the client can be held until he finds what is needed.

Therapists will either be employed directly by the GP surgery through primary health care trusts or be on self-employed contracts. It is important to have some clarity about lines of responsibility and professional indemnity. Fees paid do seem to vary quite considerably but most trusts now have experience of negotiating with therapists. The pay may not seem high but this is compensated by the benefits of working in a team and learning from colleagues and patients in a medical setting.

An interesting and useful book to refer to would be *Clinical Counselling in Medical Settings* by Peter Thomas, Susan Davison and Christopher Rance (Thomas et al., 2001).

The voluntary sector

Many therapists work in the voluntary sector, either in paid employment or as volunteers. It is a vibrant part of the therapy world that has allowed many therapists to get excellent experience which could not have been gained elsewhere. Where therapists are not paid they are usually provided with good supervision and support. If the work takes a therapist into new areas, or provides interesting colleagues, building up this sort of expertise may be more valuable than the small amount of money one might earn for working a few hours more. To work in these settings the therapist has to understand the concept of mutual benefit. The therapist may wish to work with those who are socially disadvantaged or who have a particular type of difficulty, and the agency has clients who need seeing and cannot pay much. The therapist agrees to see the clients in exchange for the agency providing support and sharing experience. The level of monitoring is likely to be quite high because voluntary therapists are given opportunities which elsewhere they would be denied without qualifications and experience.

Therapists who see money as the way their value is measured will not enjoy the voluntary sector because money is, at least partially, taken out of the equation. There are paid workers but they are usually not paid well, and frequently work hours beyond those they are paid for. Most clients are still asked to pay what they can. Therapists can experience difficulty in asking clients for financial contributions when they are not themselves being paid. People only stay in unpaid work while they are getting something out of it, which means the agencies have to provide a collegiate atmosphere, interesting clients or good supervision for their volunteers.

Agencies such as Relate, London Marriage Guidance, youth counselling services and local counselling services do a vast amount of useful work and can generate significant loyalty among the practitioners. Where management committees or co-workers fail to understand the needs of an agency and its practitioners, strong emotions can be stirred up and expressed in a way that they might not otherwise be in paid employment. A nine-to-five attitude may not be appropriate in the voluntary sector, where the work is often seen as a collaborative venture with everyone engaged in the struggle of the agency. This can be an exciting time of democratic participation, or chaos, depending on where you stand.

Moving from the voluntary sector to the private sector

The voluntary sector can provide a stimulating, supportive environment. Any move towards working privately is usually driven by financial concerns or a wish for greater independence and flexibility. It can be difficult to let go of the mother organization, regardless of whether it has represented a good, nurturing mother or a demanding, exploitative one. The therapist may have become identified with the values of the organization and either wish to continue supporting them or feel she is betraying the agency by leaving. If part of the therapist's commitment is to the provision of services for people who cannot afford private rates, this is difficult to fulfil in the private sector.

If the therapist has become accustomed to the voluntary organization providing the room, the clients and the supervision, she may be daunted by what needs to be done. It is particularly difficult in the beginning, when a room may have to be paid for in advance of any substantial client load. It may be possible to combine working in both the private and voluntary settings, thus retaining the sense of belonging and the support of being part of the therapeutic community, while starting something new.

A therapist, released from the constraints of an agency, enjoys new freedom and flexibility. Clients who would have faced a long wait in the voluntary sector can be seen quickly, with difficult work or shift patterns accommodated. However, as the practice builds up it becomes more difficult to maintain the level of flexibility without keeping slots unfilled. The therapist has to find ways of maintaining a realistic balance and facing the need to say 'no'. At times it is important to recognize, rather than exacerbate, some of the scheduling difficulties that clients face, while at the same time recognizing what meaning they might have in the therapeutic relationship.

Working alone can be an isolating experience and more frequent supervision is a response to this that also enhances opportunities for learning and professional development. A therapist who is used to the group supervision provided by an agency will miss learning from the work and experience of others. Opportunities to engage in training and continuing professional development will gradually emerge through establishing a network of local like-minded therapists. This referral network may become an important source of referrals and support, and come to embody the values that inform the practice. Such a network has to be administered. The collaborative effort involved in sustaining and administering a local network helps to establish trustworthy relationships, which will inform the struggle to run a private practice as an ethical business.

Working alongside other professionals

When the client is also in couple therapy

In the early days of marriage guidance, couples would not be offered counselling if one of the participants was already in individual therapy. Now, the complexity of an individual in two concurrent therapies is commonplace. It is helpful if the two therapists have a working relationship and have established a mutually satisfactory way of communicating. It is a breach of the UK Council for Psychotherapy ethical practice to accept a client for personal therapy when he is already in personal therapy unless this has the approval or support of the existing therapist and it is made clear to the patient which therapist holds clinical responsibility.

The tendency is still to keep the two therapies separate, with minimal contact between the two therapists. The couple therapist would rarely have contact with the individual therapist beyond the initial referral. Writing a letter establishing contact with the other therapist usefully acknowledges that the two therapies are linked. Where there is ongoing contact it can be complex, and detailed discussion is probably best avoided. Meaningful discussion is problematic and the trap of a triangulated transference is difficult to avoid. Christel Buss-Twachtmann asserts that in her experience, 'In all cases of concurrent therapy feelings of competitiveness, confusion about differences and conflicts of loyalty are present' (Buss-Twachtmann, 2000: 86). This may be expressed in relation to the differences in style, practice or interpretation between the two therapists. Even if one has the client's permission to talk to the second therapist it is quite possible that she will be reluctant to respond.

The suggestion for couple work might come from the individual therapist when couple issues overshadow the work. Christel Buss-Twachtmann (2000) believes that certain aspects of the individual become too lodged in the couple relationship to be available in the transference to the individual therapist. As the unconscious projective processes between the couple are made conscious in the couple therapy, and separateness is achieved, the individual therapy may be more able to progress.

An individual therapist will often refer for couple therapy at a time of crisis such as the emergence of family violence. Feelings will have become difficult to contain, and acting out and splitting are even more likely in relation to the two therapies. Tense situations can also arise where one person in a couple, both in individual and in couple work, stops the individual therapy. It can be tricky for either therapist to be sure whether this is a mature development, acting out, or an attack on both therapies.

Couple or individual therapy, which comes first?

Following an assessment which indicates that the prospective patient could benefit equally from either couple therapy or individual therapy, one might wonder which to undertake first. Individual work may seem less daunting and easier to organize but there are good arguments for recommending the couple therapy be attended to first. Social support is important in mental health, so attending to the social structure that supports the couple is important. While individual therapy may take the pressure off a relationship by providing a release for pent-up feelings, it may also draw energy away from the couple's relationship. A fragile relationship may become more turbulent while the individual therapy proceeds. Couple therapy is usually less protracted than individual therapy and can achieve considerable movement in a short period. It creates greater fluidity in the relationship, which will support the changes the individuals make in their personal therapy. It is frustrating to work with clients in individual therapy where the scope for change is limited by the constraints of their relationships. This would be one of the prime reasons for referring someone in individual therapy for couple or family therapy.

Working alongside the general practitioner

Most GPs would accept that in choosing to purchase private therapy the client is entitled to expect that they are buying confidentiality. However, GPs, who hold medical responsibility, might expect to be contacted if there were serious concerns about suicidal ideation or depression. General practitioners can find the confidentiality frustrating when patients re-enact family dynamics splitting the two carers. Penny Jacques (2000: 66–7) describes an example where an anorexic woman managed to set the doctor, the nurse and the therapist against one another. If the therapist is hoping the GP will facilitate an admission or psychiatric assessment, the GP is more likely to be favourably disposed if he has at least been aware of the therapist's involvement with the client.

Psychologically minded GPs with clients on medication welcome the opportunity to discuss the use of antidepressants with the therapist. GPs need good therapists to refer to, and one way they will get to know a therapist's work is through the therapist keeping them informed of the progress their patient is making. What they expect from a therapist will be influenced by the way local NHS psychotherapy departments communicate. While a full summary might be helpful, in practice a page of A4 or less usually suffices.

Social support

In dealing with physical illness, social support is one of the indicators for a good prognosis. Socially isolated individuals who are attending therapy can benefit from finding support outside the therapy room. Splitting is always a possibility but that can be worked with. Resourceful clients will find evening classes and other activities. However, I have on occasion made referrals to befriending agencies, which will provide the informal, more immediate support that I cannot provide to someone I am seeing once or twice a week. The Samaritans provide 24-hour cover and clients can either telephone or visit the centre. Clients with intrusive thoughts of suicide can find this provision immensely helpful. More usually it is valuable for someone who is temporarily overwhelmed by feelings following bereavement, or similar, who may simply need someone to be there and listen between sessions. Befriending can be an excellent support to the therapy.

A client who has made progress in therapy and is tentatively thinking of trying out the newly acquired skill of relating may need a safe context in which to experiment. A social skills course run by a local counselling service might provide exactly this. Workshops looking at sexual abuse or sexuality can also be helpful, provided that the therapist and client can tolerate the temporary disruption to the therapy.

What can a physical therapist contribute?

When a distressing event takes place there is both a psychological and a physical response. Often the physical reaction is to tense up and locate the stress in a particular part of the body, perhaps developing a headache or feelings of sickness. Our patients often describe their feelings in physical terms: 'I cannot let go, I have to hold myself together'. Where there is sustained exposure to difficult situations this can influence body posture, with clients perhaps adopting an aggressive stance or – alternatively – trying to become invisible and round-shouldered to avoid the anticipated trouble.

Clients gain considerable physical relief through addressing the complex psychological issues they bring us. We can see them adopting a more confident posture and looking less oppressed. However, if we take seriously the idea that there might be a bodily memory of the trauma as well as a psychological one, it may be worth visiting the physical. Once the patient has let go of the feelings around the trauma her body may be ready to unwind and undo the remaining traces of the early childhood difficulties. Clearly this is beyond the remit of the therapist and could mean a referral on.

Occasionally Alexander teachers or cranial osteopaths refer clients for therapy. Having done some good initial work, the physical therapist realizes that the client's body is not ready to let go further for fear of opening up feelings that the client is not in a position to deal with. If the two therapies can proceed alongside one another, in my experience the prognosis is much better.

Psychological therapists provide metaphorical holding. Frequently, touch is a difficult area for patients. Providing a safe place where there can be physical contact may be important. Someone who is psychologically and physically cut off from their body will have considerable reservations about engaging with anything physical. These fears are part of the counselling or psychotherapy – respected and never underestimated. If a therapeutic alliance can be forged with a good physical therapist she may be one of the first reliable figures the client has encountered outside the therapist's consulting room. It may encourage the idea that such figures do exist, and motivate the client to seek them out in their everyday life.

Mentoring

Therapists are becoming increasingly involved with mentoring and coaching. There is no doubt that a therapist's skills are useful in the process of mentoring. What is mentoring and coaching? The two terms are often used interchangeably but both help people improve their performance at work. Different styles of coaching and mentoring may be used. One is where the coach is an expert and is perceived as being able to apply that expertise to the person coming for coaching. Often this is related to coaching somebody into a new task or role. A finance director suddenly promoted and asked to chair the board might look to someone with experience of chairing numerous boards for coaching. The person coming to the coach is looking to pick up on his experience and perhaps be told what to do. The skilled coach will be able to help by being aware of how the person coming to coaching operates, and can attune his advice to the specific person. Taking a sporting analogy, I would expect my tennis coach to tell me how to hit my backhand, having taken into account my physical abilities and flexibility in my wrist.

The mentoring that is closest to therapy is focused less on role or task and more on the person. This form of mentoring aims to help somebody become more effective in work through looking at and exploring the behaviour patterns that they use at work. This may include making connections between patterns in work and the patterns in the mentee's life and early childhood experiences. For example, difficulties with authority figures in organizations, such as a senior manager, may be to do with unresolved earlier relationships with authority figures, especially fathers.

Many executives will come expecting you to provide advice on problems they are experiencing and will want your suggestions on what to do in their work. This is always more difficult to handle if you have experience in their sector as they come expecting you to act as an expert. Managing the mentee into thinking about broader issues and patterns, rather than giving advice, is a skill that a therapeutically trained mentor is well equipped to offer.

Unlike most private therapy contracts, mentoring contracts may be limited in time and be more like brief therapy. The meetings may not be as regular as weekly or twice weekly therapy sessions. The skill is to be aware that you are not undertaking therapy and sense how far any work can be taken within the contracted time. For example, if you are aware of major trauma in a mentee's life the question as to whether you can tackle it in the way you would within a more regular and longer-term therapy contract needs to be considered. It may not be appropriate and may leave the mentee vulnerable. It may be possible to work toward the mentee accepting a different form of work such as therapy, or to manage the relationship so the trauma is acknowledged in a way that minimizes the impact on the person in their work setting in a containing way.

When mentoring senior managers from particular industries or sectors it is helpful, but not essential, to know something about the industry or sector. Knowledge of how organizations work and the common cultures of the particular sectors will help to make sense of the mentee's position. It is not always as easy to separate role, task and person without this knowledge. Understanding the mentee's language is a necessary skill, and a general knowledge of organizations and sectors can help that. However, working on the person issues does not require the expertise that may be expected if you are working on role and task. The skills and knowledge required in working with the person are similar to those required in therapy – understanding together how patterns of behaviour are linked to emotional and life experiences and using the mentoring relationship to uncover these patterns and help the mentee to explore the connections. A group therapist or a family therapist will have the advantage of already being familiar with systems theory and complexity theory. Yvonne Agazarian has developed a systems-centred theory which has been usefully applied to work in organizations (Agazarian, 1997).

In private therapy it is usually the client who is paying for himself but in mentoring this may be different. If the company is paying and has sent the executive for mentoring, the company will have an interest in the success or otherwise of the mentoring. So the question is raised whether it is the company or the client that is the mentee. Usually the answer is 'both/and', not 'either/or', as you have a contract with both at the same time. The challenge is how to manage the relationship with both simultaneously. The mentee's agenda may or may not be the same as the company's. The contract that you hold is likely to be different with the mentee and the funding company. Managing the relationship with the company can be difficult whilst maintaining the confidential relationship with the mentee. This is easier if the company representative, the sending agent, is astute enough to understand that the work will involve confidentiality and does not have guaranteed results as far as behaviour change is concerned. At the outset, clarity of expectations is important. The mentor needs to avoid becoming the intermediary, between the mentee and his organization. This may come to a head when the mentee works on issues that clarify that he wants to leave the organization. If the organization accepts that this may be a legitimate outcome, then there will be no cause for concern. It may have been cheaper for them to pay for mentoring than to have a less effective senior executive in the organization for a longer period of time. However, if the sending agent does not see this as an acceptable outcome then it may test your relationship with them and have implications for future referrals.

Some mentees are sent and may not have chosen to come. They may not understand why the mentoring is necessary or may be defensive and reluctant to look at the reality of the behaviours that have led to the referral. Acknowledging the situation is probably a good place to start. During the first meeting such a mentee might be enabled to think about going back to his employers, in a less defensive mood, to clarify why he has been sent. Mentoring is sometimes used by employers who want to promote a technical executive but are reluctant to do so until personal skills are more in evidence.

In therapy the stresses are located in dependency and mental health concerns. Mentoring exposes the therapist to a different set of stressors, associated with success, failure and competition. The stress of the workplace will be brought into the mentoring relationship and the therapist needs to have the confidence to stay within her areas of competence. It is through conversation that people change their ideas and behaviour. Therapists who can access their expertise in the form of conversation have much to offer a mentee. Mentoring can be a rewarding experience for both parties. It is interesting to work with relatively successful people who are able to use the input to open up their work and make a difference, not just for themselves but also for others.

Beyond the consulting room

Many therapists have looked outside psychotherapy and counselling for additional interest and income. A number of psychotherapy institutes have sections that look at the application of psychotherapy in fields other than the clinical/mental health field in which it is rooted. There has been mixed success in the ability to sell therapy into different fields-marketplaces and if you wish to look at using your therapeutic skills and experience in a different field then it requires a change of mindset from that in place within the mental health field.

The fundamental question is: are you offering therapy or are you offering something that uses your skills but is not therapy? This means that you are willing to describe yourself as something other than a therapist. After all the years of training and emotional (if not financial) investment, losing that title may be emotionally difficult. Obviously certain titles and roles are closely allied to therapy and the transition to mentoring or being an 'employee assistance programme counsellor' is less significant.

What skills and knowledge do you have as a therapist? What skills have you developed from other roles you have been in, such as managing a team within an organization or being a trainer? It is very easy to underestimate the experiences and skills you have, because after working in the field for a length of time many key skills are so much part of you they become less recognized.

Once you identify the skills then you can begin to think how you could use these skills in work that is not therapy. It may mean moving outside the 50-minute hour or long-term work. It depends on whether you believe the skills you have can be useful outside the therapeutic structure. If you do, then it raises the question of how to break into a new area of work.

There is no easy answer to this but an initial step is to define the area of work where you believe you can apply your skills, and begin to define the service that you will be offering. Once you have decided that, then the question is to which marketplace you are intending to provide the service. It is common knowledge that it is difficult to change your service and the marketplace at the same time. So you might want to first change your service to the marketplace you are already known within. An example of this was a colleague who had been working as a family therapist in children's mental health services, with much contact with schools. On redefining his role as a consultant to managers in improving their people management skills, he was able to apply his skills within schools, which at the time were going through major management changes. He redefined his service but stayed within a marketplace to which he was connected through his therapeutic work. Again this person also did the opposite: he used some of the psychotherapy teaching that he had done on issues of change and people's response to it, in a commercial training company offering workshops to commercial organizations. In this case he offered the same service but in a different marketplace.

In joining with another world it may mean beginning to describe what you do in their terms and not the terms from the world of therapy. It is easier to join by talking their language than by expecting them to learn yours. So how much of the language of the market you want to enter do you know? An example of this is how a service offered is described. In the world of therapy it is usual to define the service by the problems you work with, such as depression or marital breakdown. In commercial organizations, however, services are described not on the basis of problems but to emphasize the benefits of any service, e.g. 'will reduce absenteeism or improve management effectiveness'. This does require being confident you can deliver the proposed outcomes!

Networking is vital, meeting friends, colleagues and others to talk about what you are doing and to begin the process of finding openings to use your skills. This may be through associating yourself with an organization already involved in working in the area that you want to work in and that you can bring a new skill-set to. Some people have been successful in changing career and leaving therapy; others have been able to combine both.

Chapter 8

Portfolio person, teacher and supervisor

Is there a teacher and supervisor in each of us? Supervision and teaching draw on our clinical skills without the dependency that client work entails, and create the possibility of a balanced workload. Good clinicians benefit in unexpected ways from developing skills beyond the consulting room, but how do we deal with the inhibitions and misgivings we experience in the transition from therapist to teacher or supervisor?

Our society no longer believes in a job for life and many therapists will have had another career before training as a therapist. Within the confines of a therapist's role it is possible to have considerable diversity. Indeed it is probably not advisable to be utterly dependent on one income stream and just see clients. Providing services for colleagues and students enables the therapist to function at a different level and express different parts of their personality. I hope, by describing my thoughts and experiences of teaching and supervising, to stimulate discussion amongst those who already teach and supervise and to encourage others to take the risk and find out whether it is something they might enjoy.

Teaching

Some people are gifted teachers but not many. I think everyone has something they could usefully share with therapists in training. Students really appreciate the qualified members who are prepared to communicate their interests and experiences. Therapy trainings debate whether to use the best teachers or to encourage a broad range of therapists to participate. It depends how training is understood: whether it is predominantly skills based, personality based or founded on a body of knowledge that has to be acquired. Not everything can be learnt on the course. The advent of continuing professional development means that space can be created in the initial training to teach students what they really need to know, rather than cramming everything in. Involving the membership in teaching is one way of encouraging qualified therapists to keep up with recent developments and carry on thinking theoretically. An effective way to learn something is to have to teach it to someone else.

Tutoring

Tutoring on a course and providing pastoral and academic support to an individual student is good preparation for teaching. One gets a realistic perspective on the anxieties students have and what makes it difficult for them to learn. While some students are highly academic, most will be struggling with new ideas. Even experienced practitioners may be feeling deskilled. The skilled tutor provides a framework in which the student can think. The tutor's role is to ensure that the students are developing confidence in their clinical skills and building a sound identity as a therapist.

Tutors contribute from their own experience of both training and practice. It is usually the place where students can raise issues about their training independently of the assessment process. Students will use the tutor to process the dynamics of their relationship to the course, their experience of the training structures and the difficulty inherent in learning. It is helpful if the tutor, without discounting real shortcomings, can normalize these feelings, give them a name, and assure the student that they are not alone in struggling with these issues. The student needs the tutor to fully understand their fears and frustrations but not to be overwhelmed by them or caught up in a splitting process of defending either the student or the course. Tutors need clear guidance on when, if ever, it might be appropriate to communicate with the training body. When serious issues arise the tutor would try to work together with the student and agree an approach to the training body that is in the best interests of the student.

Tutors read and comment on work in progress, mention improvements and give ideas on other sources of help. These might be suggested reading or an introduction to other students or staff with a particular interest in the field. The student wants to hear the tutor's thoughts but it is the student's ideas that need to remain central. Tutors are sometimes reluctant to comment on the style of a paper and the use of language for fear of undermining the student's confidence. However, the student who first has their attention drawn to these issues by the exam board will not be grateful. Learning to express oneself clearly in writing is justly part of therapy training. The purpose of the tutorials is to help students organize their work, to make suggestions and to monitor and help with progress.

Leading seminar groups

My introduction to therapy teaching was presenting a paper that I had written for my training, to student seminar groups. Of course it would have been possible for someone to pick holes in it. However, that was not what happened. I had written about something that interested me and I was open to new ideas, so it quickly became something we could explore together. Setting the paper in its context was helpful. I am sure the paper became more accessible to the students because I was able to explain why I had written it, how it linked with my clinical work, and why I thought it was important to grasp the ideas in it.

In some ways it is more difficult to be a student than a teacher. A student or someone reading a new paper is faced with an extremely complex task. Someone has suggested a paper be read. Presumably there is a good reason for doing so and the teacher has an idea of what might be gained from reading it. However, it is not always at all clear to the student which aspect to focus on and it can be quite indigestible. The teacher sets the agenda and has a completely different and much easier relationship with the paper. The teacher decides what is important about the paper. If students bring in other perspectives, that is a bonus. The students' certainty that the seminar leader knows something and has something to offer acts as a powerful projection, which all teachers benefit from. Teaching forces therapists to really understand theory and while it is easier to teach familiar theory it is interesting to teach topics that are less accessible.

It is useful to be able to spot the strategies students use to avoid challenging themselves and learning new material. A student who had read Lacan initially impressed me by asking each new seminar leader, 'What would Lacan think about the topic of the seminar?' However, I soon realized that if the student really had been interested, they would have found out and shared it with the rest of us. In practice it was a defensive manoeuvre, which put the seminar leader on the spot and avoided the student having to participate in the seminar. Every student will try to move the discussion onto the ground they feel most comfortable with, which could be clinical, intellectual or if they have not read the paper at all, their particular hobby horse. This is part of what gives seminars their richness and creativity. The seminar leader only needs to intervene when these activities are used as a defence against learning.

As a lecturer I get somewhat irritated if students have not done the recommended reading. I have tried setting very limited reading, or asking students to prepare examples from the reading or letting them know how I feel about the lack of preparation. I think the reality is that you are dependent on the culture of the course. It is not wise to rely on the students' good intentions. Somehow the washing machine always seems to need emptying just at the moment a student sits down to read. Giving the students the responsibility for preparing one seminar each ensures that at least one person reads the papers.

Interleaving classical seminars with action learning seminars helps to keep the process alive. Film clips, video material, role-plays and experiential learning take longer to prepare but the students are more likely to remember them a week later. Clear aims and objectives for the seminar help. Are the students simply being introduced to the ideas in a particular paper or are they expected to use the paper to help them develop their critical faculties? Students need to feel secure. If a different element is to be introduced, such as a group exercise, they need to be prepared for it and understand why it is being done.

Lecturing

Just when I was getting comfortable with my seminar presentations I was asked to do the same material for a lecture on a larger course. There were 150 participants; some experienced therapists, others sceptical about the every existence of the unconscious. My style until then had been to involve students in discussion and here I was faced with 40 minutes to fill on my own, without losing the audience. Having sought the advice of people whose lectures I had enjoyed I decided on the following strategy. Tell them what you are going to tell them; tell them; and then tell them what you have told them. In spite of the large number I decided that each person there was still an individual and that I would try to talk to 150 individuals rather then a mass. I gathered that 20 minutes was the most anyone could be expected to concentrate and that I had to divide the talk up into 10-minute slots to help them stay awake. Getting off to a good start seemed essential and so I made my initial overhead transparency beautiful to look at and clearly made especially for them.

Therapists know how to use their voices to hold a client and I found myself using that part of my training to connect with this audience. If someone is talking at you it is only to be expected that you will go to sleep. However, it is rather rude to go to sleep while someone is talking *to* you. If the speaker can convince the audience that they are in a relationship it helps. It is worth thinking about timing and delivery, and not being afraid to use language in an interesting way. My main task was to help the audience take in something of what was said. I had done my best during the lecture to bring the concepts alive but I needed to help them take something home with them. By then they were tired of my voice and my overhead transparencies. It needed to be something direct and visual. I produced a black bag and rummaged around, finding an object to represent each of the concepts we had discussed, e.g. a mirror we could look in, one side distorted, the other plain. This took courage on my part. Here I was lecturing to serious therapists who had paid to come on the course to improve their standing in the world of therapy and I was behaving like a magician pulling rabbits out of hats. I think what mattered was that it felt all right to me and I knew why I was doing it, and I explained to them why I was doing it.

It seems to me that in giving a lecture the more one can be oneself the better the lecture will be, whether you are serious and quiet or flamboyant and extravert. However, it does take real planning to keep them with you. The 'tell them what you are going to tell them' rule applies in the subsections of the lecture as much as to the whole. Otherwise it is like trying to read a paper with no subheadings. Of course if the audience do not want to listen there may not be much you can do about it. At one of these lectures someone brought the newspaper along and read it at arm's length, from cover to cover, while I battled valiantly to explain the finer points of unconscious communication. The first time I did the lecture I was certain I would dry up and be left standing on the stage with nothing to say. I went along prepared for anything and launched myself, thinking of Sisyphus pushing the stone. To my surprise there wasn't an immovable stone for me to contend with. In reality I was in front of a group of people who had been trained to sit still, listen, ask polite questions and clap at the end. What most amazed me was that when I could not answer their questions they took that as absolutely fine and they would go away and think about it some more. Suggesting they catch me over coffee rather than taking up everyone's time now usually satisfies more persistent questioners. In a group of that size communicating at all is difficult; understanding one another is maybe asking too much.

Teaching is quite a high status, if low pay, occupation and so it is worth preparing one lecture well. It can be presented once a year or there may be a number of courses that would like the input. It is of course all good marketing because people who like the way a therapist talks and thinks will want to send clients or come for supervision.

Training committees

Teachers and supervisors get drawn into committees that are concerned with training. Committees are discussed in detail in the chapter on 'Engaging with professional structures' (Chapter 9). Teachers become involved in planning the curriculum, implementing new ways of learning and monitoring students' progress. In public, and in committees, teachers nod sagely and talk about the need to raise standards and increase requirements. In private they worry about the stress the students are under, the length of the training and how everything has changed since 'my day'. These concerns should inform both our dialogue about training and what we demand of ourselves. Those suggesting that requirements be eased can be quickly shamed into silence. In the absence of any other measure, the value of the profession is measured by the length and arduousness of the training. Courses with long hours and high cost are associated with a high value tag. However, therapists undertaking rigorous therapy training at the same time as holding down a job can experience an uncomfortable identification with overstretched junior doctors.

There seems to be an irresistible pull to increase standards. Members of committees need to be alert to the new-broom tendency that frequently results in higher demands, which are not to be confused with a better quality of training. Student representatives on committees have an amazing ability to collude with extra demands placed on them. If they think something is missing from the course they want it added in, often for next year's students. After all their hard work they are determined that the course should be the best possible. If a topic is removed from the curriculum they become extremely anxious and reluctant to lose it, for fear of a gap in the training.

So how do trainings get longer and longer? A student or a staff member comes up with a good idea that will meet the needs of the immediate cohort or particular students and takes it to a committee. It is enthusiastically adopted but nothing is dropped from the curriculum, it is squeezed in. Gradually the rules around it are drawn more tightly and it becomes an increasingly arduous task. It is probably applied to all students regardless of educational indicators. As time goes by it becomes an established part of the curriculum and it is not dropped, even if the need it was meeting is less pressing. The new workload becomes normalized until the next time. Before long someone hears of an innovation on another course, which the course must keep up with and implement, and the cycle starts again. The UK Council for Psychotherapy (UKCP) has played a role in this but it is only a member organization made up of our representatives and it reflects the culture of its member organizations.

Supervision

Becoming a supervisor provides a good balance to doing clinical work. It allows a therapist to continue learning, while spending an hour exercising a different kind of concentration. It is still quite demanding but it is usually stimulating and, while it draws on emotional reactions, the supervisor is not required to be emotionally available in the same way as a therapist with a client. There are excellent books and courses on how to supervise. It is not possible to summarize these and do justice to them. I can, however, describe what it feels like to be a supervisor. I hope those readers already supervising will recognize some of the experiences I describe, and that those who would like to become supervisors will be enabled to approach the courses and books in a realistic and hopeful frame of mind. Hawkins and Shohet (2000) have written an excellent general book on supervision and Sharpe (1995) has written specifically about group supervision.

Even the most experienced therapists need someone to consult from time to time. When a case is discussed with a colleague what is looked for? Occasionally it will be some particular knowledge or experience. More usually what is needed is someone who will listen attentively, understand the difficulty and throw light on the case from a different perspective. Frequently all that is required is confirmation that the therapist is dealing reasonably well with difficult emotions which would be tricky for anyone to handle, along with some encouragement and support to carry on the work.

Becoming a supervisor is a unique experience for each of us. Our style is likely to be influenced by the best supervision we have received and our innate personalities. Those counsellors who are comfortable with 'knowing what needs to be done' will face different challenges from those who tend to the 'non-directive and unassertive' end of the spectrum. Conducting the first supervision session is probably as nerve-racking as seeing the first client. I think it is a mistake to go into the session wondering whether we can meet the needs of the supervisee. We probably cannot in the same way as we (inevitably) occasionally disappoint our clients. A more useful question might be: 'How can this supervisee be helped to get his or her needs met?' This keeps the supervisees' needs at the centre of our thoughts, and means that if nothing else he or she will feel listened to.

Supervising is a considerable responsibility and there is an element of learning from experience. This may increase anxiety levels and contribute to the supervisor feeling deskilled. It is important to stay with the not-knowing and develop some real understanding of the process. Who is being supervised? Supervising a colleague in a peer supervision group brings up completely different dynamics from supervising a trainee with his or her first client under supervision. Each makes different demands. The respect and sensitivity between colleagues in a peer group has a particular quality, which encourages openness but is mindful of individual sensibilities. In more formal supervisory situations the power relationship and tendencies towards idealization or denigration will be more obvious but can be tricky to manage. Supervisors who are experiencing some discomfort at having to supervise may not feel able to be firm enough to hold the boundaries. They may also be unwilling or unable to actively structure and hold the relationship. Experienced supervisors often revisit this experience when asked to supervise someone who is senior or very experienced in another field of therapy but looking for supervision in a specialist form of therapy where he or she is inexperienced.

An alternative response to insecurity is to become over-involved, wanting too much information or rigidly following a promising line of enquiry. It is easy to get into a stuck position through being too prescriptive. There is a powerful, shared dynamic between the supervisor and supervisee and I do not think it is surprising if we feel impulses to control or to act out. If we can resist them, they provide a rich source of information to reflect on the supervision work. It takes time to develop sensitivity to handling delicate issues, thereby avoiding lurching into therapeutic or didactic mode too easily. Sharing knowledge and expertise can enable the supervisee to develop; however, this is easily confused with baffling the supervisee with theory or getting lost in the subtle lure of the distracting, beautiful, theoretical ideas. Issues of responsibility can be tricky and we can easily find ourselves mistakenly taking responsibility for the client.

The supervision setting

Peer supervision

Now that supervision is mandatory for BACP (British Association for Counselling and Psychotherapy) Accredited Counsellors and Psychotherapists, there is a greater demand for supervision, and therapists also have more experience of being supervised. Being part of a peer supervision group is an excellent way to gain experience of supervising another's work and of observing the supervision process. It requires a considerable degree of trust among the members. Careful selection of those who are comfortable working together is important. A clear commitment to put the time aside is also essential.

Supervising trainees

A supervisee at the beginning of her training is likely to depend on the supervisor's perceived expertise and know-how. This can be disconcerting for the supervisor who has never met the client and realizes that the supervisee is in a much better place to see what is happening. Therapists in training initially feel deskilled and there is little the supervisor can do to assist with this, apart from helping the trainee to understand that it is a normal part of the process and that they as a supervisor have confidence in the trainee. The supervisor needs to accept this initial dependency and then, as the trainee grows in confidence, help them to use the supervision in a different way such that the supervisor is a resource rather than an authority. During the supervision process both partners are working out how to get the best from each other. If mutual respect can be generated the trainee will feel empowered to acknowledge that it is she who knows the client and is in charge of the therapy.

Angela Molnos (1998) describes how supervision can become excessive and after a while counterproductive:

> The trainee therapist sits facing her first patient and her mind is running on three distinct tracks at the same time or, better, jumping between them in quickly alternating sequences. One: she is listening, observing the patient, observing her own feelings, sifting through, evaluating, processing, and reacting to the incoming information. Two: as she is anxious and terribly insecure, she cannot help but try to observe herself as she presumes she appears and sounds from outside, as seen from the patient's position. Third: as this vision of herself fails to reassure her, her mind attempts to follow the whole therapeutic encounter, from the supervisor's critical observing position hovering over her and the patient. What would the supervisor say in this moment?

Supervisors are in a powerful position in relation to the trainee, and powerful transference relationships are set up. The kindest and most benevolent supervisor can be mistaken for a difficult-to-please teacher if the trainee brings those expectations to the relationship. If the supervisor can be alert to these projections she can monitor whether it is something the supervisor needs to think about in herself or whether it is something that can be worked through slowly and delicately with the supervisee. Supervision is a setting where it is very easy for malignant mirroring to occur and if a trainee has gone as far as she can with a particular supervisor there may be good arguments for a change of supervisor rather than the supervisory relationship coming to dominate and limit the training. In my experience, where a change of supervisor has been worked through slowly and thoughtfully the students have been able to move on. The student would need to reflect on and work through the difficulties before completing the training. Where students were not enabled to move, and endured an unsatisfactory supervision, the resentment may still be there years later.

A therapist coming to supervision has to reveal her vulnerability in order to get the assistance she desires. It takes considerable strength of character to put oneself in this position. Supervisors in return need to be particularly alert to their own sadistic or denigrating impulses and treat supervisees with the same level of compassionate thoughtfulness and respect that they extend to their patients. Supervisees can be just as defensive and contrary as our clients and need the same careful, painstaking attention.

Students may be in dual supervision if they have supervision both on the placement and on the training course. This has the potential to be rewarding or destructive. The supervisor has a role in helping the student to manage any potential conflict but is not well placed to do so. However, if the supervisor is able to talk about it openly and encourage the student to mention any discord, the student may do so. The simplest solution is where the student is clear which issues belong in which supervision setting. Issues relating to medical responsibility could go to the hospital, and dynamic issues to the course. Of course life is never that simple. Communication between the placement and the course helps, as does a sense that it is the student who is responsible for the therapy, not either supervisor. Where two supervisors seem to be offering contradictory insights and advice, if the story can be thought about as a whole, there is usually a way of squaring the circle, with the two interventions encompassed in a third. However, at the beginning of the discussion it rarely looks promising and the supervisor may have to concentrate hard to avoid becoming competitive with the other supervisor. Of course another way through is to understand it in terms of the dynamic between the client and the therapist, which is being acted out as a communication to the supervisors.

Supervision is the place where the theory and the clinical work come together. If I am supervising a trainee my concern is not just with the nature of the therapy the client is receiving but also with what the trainee is learning from the experience. If we are approaching a classic analytic event such as a break, I find ways to play with the idea before the student is faced with it and share my experience of how the relationship with the break is not a static one but something that varies with the history of the client and the length of the therapy. We might do a role-play. I take opportunities to talk about wider clinical issues or introduce relevant theoretical concepts. If I know a student is presenting a seminar on defence mechanisms I might suggest we look at the clinical material from this perspective.

Someone new to supervising trainees may put all kinds of unnecessary burdens on themselves. One of the most common is that they should know all about every theoretician the students will meet, on the course and off. 'You have obviously been thinking about it. Tell me how you understand it', is my usual response to a difficult theoretical question. A supervisor who feels safest on academic ground, on the other hand, may be tempted to engage in a fascinating dialogue about the theoretical ideas stimulated by the clinical material. While it appears to gratify the student, if the student is clinically weak it may be that at this stage they need to keep things very simple. Under stress a new student who is academically strong will retreat to hide behind theoretical ideas rather than using them to get closer to clients. It is important that the supervisor is not intimidated by this and understands what is happening.

Students predominantly present material as process reports. However, different ways of presenting the material give the supervisor a different perspective and I am always keen for variety. I encourage students to think of different ways to take notes of the session. Maybe they will record primarily their own countertransference or will follow a particular theme or a dream in the material. I found Patrick Casement's ideas in his book *On Learning from the Patient* (1990) helpful as a supervisor. If the therapist and supervisor together read a small verbatim section of process material from a session it is sometimes possible to see where the client is offering the therapist supervision. It is usually immensely revealing. This may mean listening to primary process communications or simply taking what the client says at face value. Some clients can communicate issues that do not feel right in the therapy directly. Others will use displacement, and discuss another figure in their life, describing an event that parallels their experience of the therapy, but not making the link. They may unconsciously try to help the therapist to understand what they need by describing someone who the therapist could learn from. Perhaps most difficult to spot is where the client identifies with, and introjects, an aspect of the therapist and then blames himself for something which could be more meaningfully understood as referring to the therapist. If the supervisee provides a very short but accurate verbatim report it is one way the supervisor can hear the client speak without the interpretation of the therapist.

Supervisors have to draw on their reserves of calm when it is difficult to see what is going on in the therapy or when it looks like the therapist might be unconsciously colluding with an unhelpful dynamic. In such a situation one often has to contain the anxiety, be supportive and wait until the therapist is in a place where they can think differently about what is happening.

Supervising a therapist working in private practice

A therapist approaches a supervisor with expectations, which are rarely matched by reality. Therapists are not immune to ideas of status and reflected glory and like to be able to say someone eminent supervised them. The new supervisor may have come highly recommended or may simply be offering the cheapest fees. Either way dynamics will follow. It is not uncommon for a potential supervisee to seek out an analytically trained supervisor and then complain when most of their interventions take that form, rather than that of the school the supervisee is more used to working in.

I take great care at the initial interview to understand what a therapist wants from supervision, why me, why now and what their previous experience of supervision is. I try to convey an idea of how I like to work as a supervisor, at the same time as assessing whether we are likely to form a good working alliance. I ask about the setting that the therapy takes place in since I need to be confident of the support structure around it. I make it clear that I am offering supervisory consultation and do not accept managerial responsibility.

Supervising a therapist working in an agency

Sometimes the therapist is bringing not only their caseload but also their responsibilities for the agency that employs them. This needs to be clear from the beginning. I do not have any management qualifications and do not claim to have. I tend to employ a systems theory approach to thinking about institutional dynamics, for example how the staff group re-enact the client group's dynamic. It is striking how staff in an adolescent unit reflect the behaviour of the rebellious young adults they work with, and those working with the elderly are preoccupied with counter-dependency. If the supervision can identify the underlying dynamic or the projections in operation between individuals, the therapist or manager can usually find a way to deal with the issues.

If it is the agency and not the therapist who is paying, then I clarify where my lines of responsibility lie. I do not see it as my responsibility to communicate with the agency if there are areas of concern; however, I would take responsibility for raising these issues with the supervisee and advising her to approach the agency. As psychotherapy and counselling become increasingly accountable professions any supervisor needs to ensure that their behaviour conforms to the latest ethical guidelines.

Group supervision

Group supervision is 'widely practiced and poorly understood' (Prieto, 1996). Gill Jones researched *Group supervision: What can go wrong?* (Jones, 2000) following an unpleasant experience herself. She suggests attention needs to be paid to the power imbalance, bullying, self-censoring of material and the imposition of group supervision by agencies. She recommends better preparation for both the supervisee and the supervisor. Chris Rose (2001), on the other hand, writes eloquently on the multilayered connections that inform and enrich a supervision group. She sees the supervisor's task as finding a way for the supervision group to express itself. This means the supervisor thinking 'group' as well as 'individual', and asking herself what is going on for the group at any particular moment, e.g. 'Is there something in this group that makes it hard to challenge men?'

The creative experience of supervising a group of therapists can be enjoyable and rewarding. Often what one therapist discusses resonates with difficulties another is experiencing. It is helpful to have a range of experiences. A newly qualified therapist will gain in confidence by listening to an established practitioner continuing to question his or her own practice. The experienced therapist, even if somewhat jaded, benefits from the enthusiasm of the newcomer. If the supervision group is within an agency it can help to build confidence between the practitioners and ensure a certain level of communication.

The fears associated with group supervision are usually around scapegoating. The supervision group is dealing primarily with feelings the supervisees find difficult to contain and work with. These uncomfortable feelings can unconsciously take root in the supervision group and find a home in whichever member is most receptive to feeling them. This practitioner will start to talk of herself as, for example, inadequate or anxious. At this level the supervisee can be seen as giving voice to something in the group. If it is recognized as such it adds to the supervision and can be reflected on. If it is denied by the other members the possibility of scapegoating arises. What is essential is that the supervisor does not collude in this process. I would wonder aloud whether the supervisee expressing concern was the only person who was feeling anxious and indicate that I thought there was cause to feel anxious. In this way I identify with the scapegoat and indicate that I do not believe the feelings belong only to her. Scapegoating primarily occurs where feelings cannot be contained and have to be evacuated. Rather than worrying about scapegoating my advice is to concentrate on developing the group into a flexible, coherent container. This means the supervisor being aware of his or her relationship with each individual and the group, thus avoiding blatant favouritism, splitting and scapegoating. The BACP now expects that anyone accredited as a supervisor of groups of therapists will have had some training in group work. This goes some way towards acknowledging that conducting supervision groups is a skill in itself.

Clearly negotiated boundaries are helpful. The supervisor usually holds the time boundary. Supervisees who feel they have not received the attention they need will be dissatisfied. Time can disappear in a myriad of ways. The dynamics of a supervision group can be fascinating and need attention. However, the supervisor can easily be diverted into dwelling too much on the group dynamic to the detriment of the supervision work and the frustration of the participants. As with all group conducting, a light touch and a genuine interest in what people have to say is probably invaluable.

At regular intervals I encourage the supervision group to give one another, and me, feedback about how we are doing as individuals and as a group. If I am allowing an unhelpful dynamic to develop in the group, the group can bring it to my attention. Also members of the supervision group can take responsibility for what they want to get out of the group and whether or not they are getting it.

Telephone supervision

With the advent of telephone conference calls it is possible to do group or individual supervision over the telephone. In my experience it works well for people who are comfortable talking on the telephone. Therapy is no longer the preserve of those living in Hampstead and, with the premium on time and travel, telephone supervision seems destined for increased use. Telephone conference calls have revolutionized the possibilities for group supervision over the telephone. I think it is helpful if the group occasionally meet in person. Fantasies can be kept in check and the level of trust and reflection deepened by contact. Video conferencing will be even better but in the meantime anyone doing telephone conferencing needs to develop his or her own version of 'over and out'. Without the visual clues it is impossible to distinguish a reflective silence at the end of a sentence from the end of what someone has to say. As soon as someone says, 'I wonder what you think?' everyone knows where they stand.

Online supervision

Over recent years information technology has become an increasingly important part of counselling and psychotherapy. There are many ways that technology can be used in therapeutic work, including email, Internet relay chat, discussion boards, telephone video link and stand-alone software packages. Where clients are less able to access traditional face-to-face meetings with their therapist there is clearly potential for these methods. An international research project is looking at the provision of online supervision from a website which links those looking for online supervision with those willing to provide it. This website, www.online-supervision.net, has a discussion forum, academic resources, links and a description of the research, and is intended as a focus for anyone interested in using technology to access or provide supervision.

The technology can be applied in individual therapy, groups, supervision and training. Like other forms of delivery of therapy, practitioners need to be proficient and able to ensure that what we offer is both effective and safe. Those who tread unwarily are liable to the pitfalls of these innovative methods where they are poorly or improperly delivered. Kate Anthony and Stephen Goss provide a

comprehensive guide to the ethical, theoretical and practical consid-
erations for practitioners, alongside case studies, in their book
Technology in Counselling and Psychotherapy: A Practitioner's Guide
(Goss and Anthony, 2003). They also describe the likely impact of
these technologies on therapeutic relationships and the outcomes that
can be expected. Consultancy and training within the area of technology in therapy are available at www.onlinecounsellors.co.uk and
www.kateanthony.co.uk; supervision at www.online-supervision.net.

What am I thinking about when I am supervising?

My relationship is with the supervisee, not with the client, and I make
it clear that any ideas I have are for the therapist to think about, not
to act upon. My nightmare as a supervisor is the supervisee who takes
everything I say and transfers it wholesale into the session with the
client. I make it clear to supervisees that I will only feel free to be open
about what I think if I know they will do what they think is right in
the session, regardless of what I say.

In order to supervise I need some minimum structure. I need a good
description of the client's family history, a description of their relationship with the supervisee, and a description of the session or part
of it. The discussion frequently moves in unexpected directions, but at
the beginning of listening to material I find it helpful to know what the
therapist is concerned about or interested in. This avoids the deeply
frustrating experience of listening to lengthy material from one perspective, only to discover that the supervisee's interest lies somewhere
entirely different. It also encourages supervisees to do some processing
of the material before they come so that I am moving them forward,
rather than simply doing work they could have done themselves with
a little effort. As a supervisor I am looking for patterns and relationships as well as the forces that might influence these connections. It is
similar to the process model of supervision which Hawkins and
Shohet (2000) describe and which they appropriately call the Seven-
Eyed Supervisor Model.

Supervisors have a particular role when therapists are going
through stressful life events. In cases of illness it is the supervisor's job
to manage practitioners' anxieties and help them make the best possible arrangements without falling into denial or masochistic
behaviour. Holding and containing are key elements of supervision.

Section 4

Professional roles

Engaging with professional structures
Why isn't counselling and psychotherapy a force to be reckoned with?
Why bother with audit and research?
Committee work
Disciplinary complaints

Chapter 9
Engaging with professional structures

The world of therapy is ambivalent about becoming a profession and the change this involves. We want the advantages but despair of the control, which threatens the radical nature of therapy. Creative, clinically sound therapists can influence the development of the profession and lessen the narcissistic injury implicit in the transition to the new professional practices. Audit, complaints procedures and committee work are at the heart of these new structures.

Why aren't counselling and psychotherapy a force to be reckoned with?

In the 1970s and 1980s the world of counselling and psychotherapy was thought of as rather odd, and easily confused with scientology and brainwashing. Now it is integrated with the academic world. The lady amateur has given way to the career woman and the scientist practitioner largely replaces the pastoral therapist. Psychotherapy and counselling are vigorously promoted by National Health Service trusts as an alternative to medication. The Department of Health booklet *Treatment Choice in Psychological Therapies and Counselling: Evidence Based Clinical Practice Guidelines* (Department of Health, 2001) describes psychological therapies that should be offered, and on the basis of evidence recommends types of therapy. It also insists on audit to ensure the recommendations are acted on.

Ever more complex structures are evolving to support or control these developments. Whether we arrive at a position where the tail is wagging the dog will be determined by the personality traits of the people who are attracted to work on psychotherapy and counselling bodies. The type of people attracted to committees will determine the shape of the profession in the future. Unfortunately office holders often bring an unhelpful fit between their characterological traits or difficulties and the office they hold, e.g. the apocryphal treasurer who is of course mean and controlling.

Most therapists want a quiet life and the prevalent culture is one of unwillingness to engage in risk-taking behaviour. In isolated corners of the profession someone is unconsciously delegated the task of risk assessment and planning for the future, but generally she receives little thanks, support or recognition. More commonly therapists engage in fantasies of 'a new building' and 'recognition for their brand of therapy' with everyday conversation centred on 'if only we could ...' or 'if only we had ...'. Therapists have a tendency to catastrophize or adopt ostrich-like behaviour when dealing with change, and retreat to the consulting room.

Given the number of people trained as therapists, our influence should far outweigh that of psychologists, yet they hold the positions of influence. Psychologists have claimed a scientific validity for their activities. Evidence-based practice rules OK. Therapists have not carried out enough efficacy studies. However, there are difficulties. Controlled trials may not relate to the real world. Therapists deal with relationships and individuals, not with symptoms. How do you measure these? It is going to be very important how psychotherapy and counselling research develops and whether we can find ways to study therapy with complex and diffuse outcomes.

The failure of the psychotherapy and counselling profession to develop into a health service profession has played into the hands of the psychologists. Clinical psychology is seen as developed from science whereas therapists are often arts students, and – in a world where medicine dominates the culture – psychotherapy and counselling are more difficult to accommodate. Psychotherapy and counselling, by remaining outside the juggernaut, remained a cottage industry with no substantial infrastructure. Disagreements prevented registration. There would have been losses if psychotherapy and counselling had become part of the NHS machine, but there is a certain security in being given training in resuscitation, finance, computer skills, management skills, data protection, equal opportunities and interviewing techniques, all of which are bread and butter to NHS staff. While we may not be interested in most of the above, they do equip a practitioner to deal on equal terms with people from other professions.

Psychoanalysis and medicine provided the roots of psychotherapy and determined the culture. It is worth taking a critical look at the shadow side of this culture. Medicine was set up in such a way as to prevent free trade. Doctors were not allowed to advertise and even now they can only cite qualifications and say what they do. They cannot claim any special skill or claim to be better than others. This prevents clients finding out for themselves who is good at what. The lack of information is presented as protecting clients but in practice it protects practitioners from having to size up their own strengths and weaknesses. Therapists occupy a similar position, which is likely to be challenged.

It is interesting and disturbing to note that at the same time as practitioners are being made more accountable, accusations of inappropriate sexual behaviour and abuse by doctors and therapists are coming out of the woodwork. In the 1980s, society was shocked to discover the level of hidden sexual abuse that had been going on in families. It is possible we will have to live through a period of discovering the level of sexual activity which has been hidden behind the closed door of the surgery and consulting room.

Why bother with audit and research?

Audit may seem an unfamiliar term in therapy. However, we are a reflective profession, and informal qualitative audit has always been part of our tradition. Professionalization carries with it a demand for slightly more concrete audit. I am concerned here with simple audit (rather than in-depth research) and the development of evidence-based practice. What information is collected depends on why the therapist is carrying out the audit and what she wants to know. A basic record which lists the historical facts of the practice can be used as a record of the workload, provide evidence for feedback to clients, and form the basis of income analysis (Figure 9.1).

Each therapist needs to develop his or her own list and to keep it to the essentials. If the information is in number form, one year can be compared with another and averages and percentages can be identified. Thus I might be interested in how much of my work is short term or long term, or whether the average fee I am charging is what I would

Name ....

Date of initial contact ....

Start of therapy ....End of therapy ....

Length of therapy ....

Fee paid ....

Type of therapy ....

Outcome:

Dropped out   Could have stayed on   Finished

Referred by:

Self   General practitioner   Colleague

Name of referrer ....

Figure 9.1 **Basic data for audit**

hope for. Equally if I only have one referral from a GP, I might decide either to give up on GPs as a source of referrals, or that I am neglecting them and try to meet more.

When working with students in an agency, I looked at what times of the year the service had the most clients. The service was busiest in November, and quietest in the summer exam period. This was helpful information. It allowed therapists to say to troubled students in November that it was not unusual to get depressed at that stage of the university life cycle. It also helped to contain the anxiety of a busy service, which was concerned that it would not be able to cope in the exam season.

Clients are inclined to shop around and may well ask, 'How long do most people stay in therapy?' An accurate answer to that question may be different from the 'gut feeling' we have for the time. It is important we do not mislead potential clients. A therapist who is experiencing a run of dropouts may find the experience easier to deal with if she has figures that show this happens every year at a similar manageable level.

Research

Therapists practise in a world where evidence-based practice holds sway and research findings are important. While therapists will rightly resist the straitjacket of randomized controlled trials, psychodynamic psychotherapy researchers and others are rising at last to the challenges posed by formal outcome research. 'Moreover a recently published open door review of outcome studies in psychoanalysis and psychoanalytic psychotherapy testifies to the wealth of high quality ongoing studies in this domain [Fonagy et al., 1999]. These should bear fruit in the coming decade' (Richardson, 2001).

Research is emerging from the dusty corners and becoming accessible to practitioners. The British Association for Counselling and Psychotherapy has taken a lead in providing members with a quarterly journal, *Counselling and Psychotherapy Research*, which links counselling and psychotherapy research with practice. In a similar vein Leuzinger-Bohleber and Target, in their book *Outcomes of Psychoanalytic Treatment* (2002), aim to bridge the gap between practising therapists and researchers.

Committee work

The new professional structures operate through committees. It is probably not wise for the innovative, creative members of an institute to leave the committee work, and the future of therapy, to those who enjoy patrolling the regulations. Being a member of a committee can be an important part of consolidating a rounded identity as a therapist working with colleagues. Joining a committee is a complex social transaction. Is it a case of volunteering or waiting to be asked? Is there a queue of people waiting to serve or is the committee desperate for new blood? Will the volunteer be able to do what she is interested in or will a multitude of other tasks unfold? Where an election is involved, the person not selected will have difficult feelings to deal with. The work is interesting but not particularly rewarding, so there is little incentive to expose oneself to rejection. However, it has to be done.

Most therapy trainings and organizations consider themselves democratic and aim to meet the needs of their membership. It is easy to be critical or dismissive of the committee structure, which tries hard but often fails. If you want to make something happen in the world of therapy it is worth considering whether you have a greater chance of success operating within, or outside, the existing structures. If you decide to use the existing structures, take some time to understand how they work.

Decision-making

Therapists are generally fairly bright, thoughtful people, so one might not anticipate any difficulty with decision-making. However, in my experience nettles are rarely grasped and when they are, they sting. Committee members quickly learn a great deal about how to avoid making decisions. We put ourselves in a difficult position when we take responsibility for an aspect of our institute. We are often working with the nebulous idea of 'The good of the institute', with little clear idea of what would be good for the institute. Our investment in the good standing of the training institute probably exaggerates the burden of responsibility and makes us more anxious to reach the 'right' decision.

Most decision-making supports the status quo and is easily defensible if criticized by other members. If there are a number of people making a decision, what they can all agree upon is likely to be a defensive stance. This resistance to change is not conscious and each member is there to make a difference; however, this seems to be part of the group dynamic and I think it should be resisted. Every committee needs a person who does not get too involved and who manages to stay in touch with the common sense of what is being discussed. He or she can often lightly suggest a way through the polarized positions members take up.

It is hardly surprising then that decisions are routinely deferred, avoided, rescinded and not implemented. Route one is to have a full discussion and then defer the decision. This can be repeated at subsequent meetings and further information sought until the issue ceases to be of importance, or the committee becomes preoccupied with other issues. A difficult decision can be avoided altogether by referring it elsewhere, perhaps to a working party or to another committee, preferably one that is overburdened or meets infrequently.

Sticking to decisions is as difficult as making them. When you have a group of bright people, there are a hundred sophisticated ways to reintroduce a topic and arrive at a different decision. Given that either decision would probably be sustainable it seems more important to implement decisions. Most therapy organizations are risk averse but there will be pockets of innovation. These are probably the delicate growing shoots of the organizations and they can be either nurtured or trampled on. If they are too threatening to the status quo, the organization will find ways of frustrating the individuals involved and the ideas will be driven into the sand. However, often years later, they resurface and can be integrated into the mainstream. Understanding the culture in operation is essential to finding ways of influencing it in the desired direction. This may involve calculated political action or gentle coaxing.

In a defensive culture, members are disinclined to take actions or decisions without reference to a committee. Confusion can also surround what authority a committee has. Once one committee is consulted the chances are that others will want to discuss the issue. Creativity is most likely to flourish where decision-making is delegated to those who are undertaking activities. Anyone taking a decision needs to feel that they will have the backing of their organization. It is stultifying when therapy organizations embrace a conformist stance that being in line with everyone else takes precedence over innovation and originality.

One mistake in decision-making is consulting too widely and becoming confused. It may be wise to take time to think about whom to involve in a decision. Good decision-makers seem to be people who once they have made the decision feel they have achieved something and move on to the next task. Others endlessly and ineffectively review the decision and wonder whether it was appropriate. It is helpful to bear in mind that a wrong decision is not usually the end of the world, as another, different decision can then be made.

The committee as therapy session

When a group of therapists get together, all kinds of transferences and group dynamics come into play. On joining a committee one is not just new to the committee but also adapting to working with colleagues who may have been inspirational as teachers or irritating as fellow students. It would not be surprising if senior colleagues were deferred to or if disagreement was difficult. Rather than address these dynamics and expose the hidden alliances and old hierarchies, the members tend to invest in a myth that everyone is participating on an equal footing. Where frank exchange and honest communication is not encouraged, it will be more difficult for therapists to use their analytic mind to think about the issues and develop the kind of dialogue therapists rely on to make sense of issues. It is easy for a discussion to resemble a therapy session and for everyone to express their thoughts and feelings but not arrive at any conclusions. In the consulting room we have plenty of time and I think it is difficult to adjust to an idea of prioritizing the agenda and directing the meeting.

Participating in a committee

Committee members have status and privileged knowledge of what is happening in the world of therapy. Some committees have higher status than others and the perceived status does not always accord with the actual importance of the committee. Experienced members will tend to drift to the high status committees regardless of which committees they would be most valuable on.

Committee work is a serious undertaking, and if the institute is a charity the committee structure is answerable to the Charity Commissioners. Those who learn the kind of discourse needed in a committee are probably the most effective. We have to learn how to disagree creatively and argue our point so that our voice is heard. It is easy to be irritated with objections but one needs to be able to evaluate them. Is the person bringing a sound point, which has been overlooked, or are we dealing with an emotional, personal or anti-group response? Fascinating discussions take place and one learns a lot but at the end of the day it is about making things happen. We need to have the courage to take the authority, influence and responsibility a committee has, and use it.

Chairing a committee

Committees take decisions on behalf of the membership, and chairing a committee means taking authority. Committees appear to be charged with arriving at decisions but I suggest they are first negotiating disagreements. They need to recognize and work with incompatible interests and conflicts of ideology. Reconciling these is really at the heart of enabling change. It is tempting to try to bypass the difficulties or use political manoeuvring to manage the outcome; however, the difficulties simply re-emerge elsewhere. In conducting an analytic group, it is the conductor's ability to step back and think about the group's dynamics and resistances that prevents him or her being overwhelmed by the group's feelings. Therapists chairing meetings need to cultivate this skill. Like the group conductor, it is their job to carry on thinking when others get stuck in regressive, defensive behaviours. One excellent organization I worked for had an annual large group meeting with the sole topic, 'Where are we going and what are we here for?' Anyone taking decisions in any committee knew what the membership thought the organization was trying to do. When I moved on I found it extraordinary that other organizations tried to manage without it.

A meeting around a table conveys a message of getting down to business. Starting and finishing on time instils a professional discipline. Therapy sessions have a rigid time structure, which focuses the work. Adding extra time to a meeting only ensures that one spends longer going around in circles. Most of the work would probably be better done outside the committee in smaller working parties. It may be that instead of delegating work the committee is trying to do it all itself or delegating work and then constantly checking up on those entrusted with the task. How long a meeting takes depends on how well-prepared the members are and whether an informed discussion can take place. A good Chair will distribute an agenda and information ahead of the meeting, which allows each member to come with a sense of what they think and how they would like to approach the issues. If the minutes predominantly record decisions, as opposed to the detail of the discussion, it will soon become clear whether decisions are being reached or avoided. Minutes should indicate action that has been decided upon and who needs to take action. Circulating the minutes soon after the meeting helps to ensure that decisions are actually implemented.

The Chair needs to know when to be controlling and when to let people have their say. It is difficult for members to fully support decisions that they have reservations about if they do not feel they have had their chance to be heard. It can be tedious to hear everyone but in the long run it saves time. It is also important to allow the committee to make the decisions and not to fall into the seductive 'lazy committee' behaviour of rubber-stamping what the Chair wants.

The time to avoid chairing a committee is when the structure supporting it is inappropriate. If a subcommittee has more heavyweight members than the committee it is responsible to, it is unrealistic to think that accountability is going to be exercised properly. Committees frequently spend as much time demarcating their own territory in relation to other committees as they do planning for the future. Good communication between committees is essential but if many of the committee members are only there because they are on another committee it is going to be hard to find bodies to do the work of the committee. The same applies to having too many of 'the great and the good' on the committee. Their experience may well be invaluable, but it is helpful if they are also prepared to do some of the time-consuming tasks between meetings.

Difficult issues in committees

The most difficult job a committee has is saying 'no' to a colleague. Selection runs all the way through therapy organizations. We select our students, our supervisors, our teachers and our committee members. We also have to choose which projects an institute can undertake and how we want to operate. Someone has to say 'yes' or 'no' at each of these junctures.

It is easy to say 'yes', difficult to say 'no'. It is also difficult to hear 'no'. Some people when told 'no' will ignore it and carry on anyway; others will withdraw hurt and silently punish the rejecting institute. It is not easy to meet someone from the panel who turned you down, or someone you turned down. Committee members will only say 'no' if they feel they will be supported and if they feel they have been given the tools they need to make the decision. It is difficult to have confidence in our decisions if the committee starts to become a clique or if a small clique starts to dominate discussions. Clear criteria that all parties are aware of will lessen the likelihood of misunderstanding. Naturally the real reason I am anxious about saying 'no' to you is that you may then say 'no' to me one day. Everyone saying 'yes' to everyone else seems a seductive option. Of course, it is just as unhelpful when people get into the habit of saying 'no' and all concerned become despondent and give up hope of doing anything new and moving forward.

Disciplinary complaints

It would be comforting to think that disciplinary hearings only happen to other people. Unfortunately the increasingly litigious attitude in wider society renders this unrealistic. Most people will know someone who has been the subject of a complaint, and where it is upheld, it is always difficult to believe the colleague could have been so naïve, rash, careless or abusive. Realistically it illustrates the powerful dynamics we are engaged with and the importance of ethical practice. It could happen to any one of us. It may be our own deliberate fault, but also misunderstandings do happen and we cannot protect ourselves from malicious complaints. In therapy, difficulties sometimes arise rather like accidents. There is little conscious malice or neglect but misunderstandings easily become magnified by bad luck or bad timing, and the crumpled bodywork has to be dealt with.

The shock that inevitably accompanies receipt of a formal complaint is not unlike that of the aftermath of an accident. Anger, fear and grief are normal responses. While prevarication is not to be advised it may be sensible not to react immediately but to consult a supervisor or a friend, while allowing a few days for the initial surge of overwhelming feelings to subside before submitting a formal response. Early contact with the professional indemnity insurers is useful as many have helplines and excellent advice.

Casemore (2001) provides further guidance about dealing with complaints.

Beware the lure of openness

Therapists are trained to be open and to share with colleagues in a variety of settings. We look beyond the obvious and acknowledge unconscious shadow aspects of the personality. This can lead therapists in disciplinary procedures to create problems for themselves by saying so much that they talk themselves into jail (metaphorically only, one hopes). What matters are the facts, not the interpretations. It is usually wise to answer the questions asked and not muddy the waters with explanations. Therapists who are used to exploring every facet of a difficulty can unconsciously collude with a panel to make a mountain out of a molehill. Both the complainant and the therapist complained against tend too much to pursue ramifications and explanations. Any panel will appreciate clarity of focus, as against obfuscation with a mass of peripheral detail.

The mere suggestion of impropriety can inflict a narcissistic injury. As therapists we know ourselves fairly well, but we still need to guard against the common responses to a disciplinary accusation. It is easy to respond to a complaint angrily and defensively, seeing only the unfairness and the insult. Typical responses might be 'How dare anyone suggest ...' or 'Who do they think they are to throw stones?' Another version embraces denial and asserts that the complaint has nothing to do with the therapist and that whatever is complained of would have happened anyway. This is the 'What, me?' approach. It is particularly likely in colleagues who have worked hard to establish a good reputation. I don't think it is surprising if we use projection and denial to deal with a persecutory situation. However, it can make it hard for the therapist involved to think about what has happened and may limit her ability to manage the disciplinary hearings creatively.

The other extreme is the 'Nail me to the hillside' approach. The practitioner puts her hands up immediately. She feels dreadfully guilty without thinking whether she was responsible or could have done anything different in the circumstances. 'Of course it is all my fault, how could I have been so stupid?' Alternatively, in a misguided wish to get it all over with, they identify with the aggressor: 'If I am in this position I must have done something, and I am sure it will turn out to be my fault so I might as well admit it now and get it over with.' We have all been taught not to immediately admit liability in a car accident and a similar reticence in disciplinary procedures would probably be helpful.

The disciplinary procedure

Disciplinary enquiries are interested in the therapist's professional practice. Like it or not, a disciplinary hearing is a legal, political and social undertaking. The therapist needs to be present throughout the proceedings. It may be unpleasant but others will find it much more difficult to be critical or get caught up in inappropriate dynamics with the therapist there. One of the most trying aspects of this process is the sheer length of time it can take. Therapists under accusation often seem unable to think of anything else. It dominates their lives, sometimes for a year or more. Therapists may sometimes look for a therapeutic context in which to explore and discharge the welter of feelings provoked. Others, feeling their privacy is already intruded upon, may depend on advisers, family and friends to sustain them.

Each regulatory body has its own process but a typical one would involve:

- a panel to see if there is a case to answer;
- a panel to hear the complaint;
- a panel to hear any appeal;
- further appeals by either party if dissatisfied with any aspect of the procedure.

The simplest complaint can drag on for years, although procedures are designed to try and achieve a fair hearing as rapidly as possible. Fiona Palmer Barnes gives excellent advice and information in *Complaints and Grievances in Psychotherapy* (Palmer Barnes, 1998). She introduces ideas around ethics, competence, contracts and confidentiality and goes on to describe how complaints procedures work in practice. It is an immensely practical book and includes sample letters that can be written in the event of a complaint.

One example she gives is of a letter arriving from a client who has dropped out, complaining about recent sessions and asking for a refund of fees. This could be the beginning of a direct complaint from the client. The response needs to be conciliatory and demonstrate understanding of what the writer has written. On the other hand, it is important that the practitioner at no stage accepts responsibility for poor professional practice. It may be that the letter from the client is written in the spirit of wanting to be heard, to have the hurt feelings acknowledged and to protect other clients from what is seen as insensitive treatment. Fiona Palmer Barnes offers the following letter as an example of what might be an appropriate response.

Dear

I understand that you felt that the last few sessions have been less than satisfactory from your point of view. I heard this in the last sessions we had together and in your letter. I had felt that your concerns had been discussed in the last sessions we had together but your letter indicates that you do not feel that the matter has been resolved. I am concerned about this.

Under the circumstances perhaps you would like to have a further session for which I would/would not make any charge so that we can discuss the matter further.

Should you feel that it would be better if this interview took place in the presence of a third party, I would be very willing to ask another colleague to come and meet us both.

(Palmer Barnes, 1998: 68; reproduced with permission)

Not all failures on the part of a therapist amount to malpractice and I found her descriptions helped to clarify the different categories.

- A mistake is an unintended slip in good practice.

- Poor practice is a failure to pay due care and attention to practice standards that the practitioner knows are required.

- Negligence is a want of proper care or attention and involves carelessness.

- Malpractice is generally defined as practice or behaviour that is intentionally emotionally, financially, physically or sexually abusive.

Choosing a friend for support

A friend is entitled to provide support at a disciplinary hearing. Choosing the person is a key decision. I am reminded of a contestant in the celebrity version of 'Who wants to be a Millionaire?'. When asked whom she would like as her 'phone a friend' friend, she chose a woman who had previously won the jackpot. They were not 'friends' but she could provide what was needed. Clearly it needs to be someone who can be trusted and confided in. However, it is a legal and political process, so whatever strengths the therapist under investigation has, the colleague needs to complement them. Approaching an eminent senior colleague may give the illusion of potency but having someone who understands the process, and how to influence it, is probably more important.

Supervision

Supervision plays an important role in helping with complaints, whether by helping avoid them or managing a difficult situation so it does not go as far as a complaint. Supervision can provide support in the face of a complaint. Many disciplinary processes offer space for conciliation and this is clearly easier in advance of a formal complaint being launched. Clients will frequently approach the training body to discover what processes are open to them. At this point creative solutions can sometimes be found which facilitate mutual understanding and resolution. In hospital settings medical clients frequently feel let down and pursue complaints procedures simply because the consultant has not understood quite how angry the client is. Doctors who are able to tolerate this anger and frustration may save the National Health Service vast sums of money by allowing the patient to express their disappointment with the way things turned out. Managing our clients' expectations and not colluding with idealization may be important in pre-empting complaints.

Legal advice

A therapist's livelihood depends on her good name and registration. Legal advice at an early stage may be useful. It is worth checking with professional indemnity insurers whether they provide cover for legal expenses in disciplinary hearings or limit it to personal liability claims in the courts. Such additional cover may cost extra but can be useful.

Serving on a disciplinary panel

Serving on a disciplinary panel is one of the more demanding roles an institute can request from one of its members. In agreeing to participate, it is essential to consider carefully whether any personal relationship exists which could compromise the proceedings. It is sometimes difficult to distinguish the role from the person. Relationships are changed by what takes place, and afterwards collegial relationships may need to be rebuilt with care. Equally the nature of the complaint is important, as is an awareness of the possibility of unconscious identifications. With powerful dynamics in play, one could understand how the dynamics of the complaint might become re-enacted in the relationships of the panel members with one another.

We can support colleagues who sit on panels by providing them with appropriate support. They need ethical guidelines that are up to date, relevant, unambiguous and workable. A suitable range of enforceable sanctions is required. The training institute is effectively rendered toothless if there are few options between termination of membership and a verbal slap on the wrist. Sanctions have to protect clients but asking someone to stop working may not be appropriate. Equally, where a sanction is intended to indicate a loss of status such as committee membership, teaching or supervision, this may be difficult to enforce and may need to be introduced over a period of time. The training organization has to back the findings of panels. It is easy for those who have not been involved in the enquiry to question the result and want to dismiss it, particularly if acting on the report will mean confronting painful issues. Those who have been on the panel will have seen a great deal of confidential information. Holding privileged information is a burden since one has to withhold it in other situations where it might be relevant.

The relationship of the panels with the rest of the training institute is crucial. High quality training is needed for both members and students, and Rosemary Kent, who works with POPAN (the Prevention of Professional Abuse Network), believes that 'Adequate training about ethical practice in the psychological therapies would not only mean that practitioners learned a great deal about their own vulnerabilities it would also instil a culture of transparency, accountability and vigilance in their professional organisations and employment environments' (Kent, 2003). If complaints were seen as 'matter of fact' and the usual way to deal with misunderstandings, it might be less damaging for the individuals involved. Instead of the gossip, side-taking and prurient interest stirred up by a rumour of an indiscretion, we might be able to move to a more open situation where the complainant and the therapist involved could be offered the support needed to participate fully. In such a climate, mediation might have a larger role and clients, and therapists, who had been through the process helped to find some resolution afterwards.

Clarkson (2000) gives helpful advice on the subject of ethical and moral dilemmas in psychotherapy.

Health

Some complaints are readily identifiable as relating to the health of the practitioner. These would be better dealt with by an informal meeting, which might come up with recommendations. If these were not adhered to, it would become a matter for a health committee to pursue and advise the professional body what action need be taken.

Reporting a colleague

A complaint by one practitioner about the practice of another can be very painful and can impact on both the individuals and the training body. This is particularly so where the colleague whose work is causing concern is an older, established and revered therapist. The knowledge of the distress that will follow can deter therapists from taking the issue up. However, where practitioners are aware of circumstances that they believe jeopardize clients if they do not act, they may be equally guilty of misconduct by not taking action. It may be that practitioners believe the normal channels of communication are no longer possible and therefore see an independent investigation as the only way to protect the reputation of the profession.

Finally

Successful therapy seems to derive, in large part, from the quality of the relationship between the therapist and the client. I think this stems from our capacity to engage with the client through an intimate part of our self. Training and experience ultimately enable us to be ourselves in the presence of the intense unbearable feelings we encounter in our clients and ourselves. Where there is authenticity, integrity and the capacity to play, each resulting relationship is unique. The profession as a whole has to remember how to play and not take itself too seriously. If we can achieve this the super ego we take into the consulting room will assist rather than limit us.

The profession is once more approaching government regulation but this time with a broader more inclusive remit. Changes that the profession has already made in terms of engaging with academic university departments will extend as therapists find ways to pursue research that genuinely informs and educates about the quality of the therapeutic relationship. If we can undertake audit, but more importantly have the conversations that the audit stimulates and ask ourselves the challenging questions we may find new possibilities. As research and academic questioning become are enshrined in the culture some sacred cows will not survive but others will find a new vitality. How the profession evolves will be determined by the conversations that happen inside and outside committees and whether we can continue to be genuinely present and think, or find ourselves lost in the assumptions others make about who we are and what we need.

References

Agazarian Y (1997) Systems-Centered Therapy for Groups. New York: Guilford Press.

Agazarian Y, Peters R (1981) The Visible and Invisible Group: Two Perspectives on Group Psychotherapy and Group Process. London: Routledge and Kegan Paul.

Anderson L (1994) The experience of being a pregnant group therapist. Group Analysis 27: 75-85.

Black R (1987) Getting Things Done: A Radical New Approach to Managing Time and Achieving More at Work. London: Michael Joseph.

Brookes S, Hodson P (Eds) (2000) The Invisible Matrix. London: Rebus Press.

Burch R (2000) What happens in a group when all the members know they are dying? (Personal communication.)

Buss-Twachtmann C (2000) Splitting and sharing in concurrent therapies. In: Brookes S, Hodson P (Eds) The Invisible Matrix, pp. 80–99. London: Rebus Press.

Butler G, Hope T (1997) Managing yourself and your time. Managing your Mind, The Mental Fitness Guide, pp. 31-44. Oxford: Oxford University Press.

Casement P (1990) On Learning from the Patient. London: Routledge.

Casemore R (2001) Surviving complaints against counsellors and psychotherapists – towards understanding and healing. In: Casemore R (Ed.) Ross on Wye: PCCS Books.

Clarkson P (2000) Ethics. Working with Ethical and Moral Dilemmas in Psychotherapy. London: Whurr.

Deben-Mager M (1993) Acting out and transference themes induced by successive pregnancies in the analyst. International Journal of Psychoanalysis 74: 129-39.

Department of Health (2001) Treatment Choice in Psychological Therapies and Counselling: Evidence Based Clinical Practice Guidelines. London: Department of Health.

Etchegoyen A (1993) The analyst's pregnancy and its consequences on her work. International Journal of Psychoanalysis 74: 141-9.

Fonagy P, Kaechele H, Krause R, Jones E, Perron R (1999) UCL Psychoanalysis Unit, London.

Goss S, Anthony K (2003) Technology in Counselling and Psychotherapy: A Practitioner's Guide. London: Palgrave.

Hale R (1991) Suicidal acts. In: Holmes J (Ed.) Textbook of Psychotherapy in Psychoanalytic Practice. Edinburgh: Churchill Livingstone.

Hawkins P, Shohet R (2000) Supervision in the Helping Professions. Buckingham: Open University Press.

Jacques P (2000) Relationships cubed. In: Brookes S, Hodson P (Eds) The Invisible Matrix, pp. 59-79. London: Rebus Press.

Jones G (2000) Group supervision: What can go wrong? Counselling 11: 648-9.

Kent R (2003) Can therapists be taught to be ethical? Counselling and Psychotherapy Journal 14: 18-21.

Leuzinger-Bohleber M, Target M (Eds) (2002) Outcomes of Psychoanalytic Treatment. London: Whurr.

Mariotti P (1993) The analyst's pregnancy: The patient, the analyst and the space of the unknown. International Journal of Psychoanalysis 74: 151–64.

McMahon G (1994) Setting Up Your Own Private Practice: in Counselling and Psychotherapy. Cambridge: NEC.

Molnos A (1995) A Question of Time: Essentials of Brief Dynamic Psychotherapy. London: Karnac Books.

Molnos A (1998) A Psychotherapist's Harvest: A to Z of Clinical Practice and Theoretical Issues. http://fox.klte.hu/~keresofi/psyth/a-to-z-entries/supervision.

Palmer Barnes F (1998) Complaints and Grievances in Psychotherapy: A Handbook of Ethical Practice. London: Routledge.

Prieto LR (1996) Group supervision. Still widely practiced but poorly understood. Counselor Education and Supervision 35: 295–307.

Richardson P (2001) Evidence-based practice and the psychodynamic psychotherapies. In: Mace C, Moorey S, Roberts B (Eds) Evidence in the Psychological Therapies: A Critical Guide for Practitioners, pp. 157–73. London: Brunner-Routledge.

Rogers C (1994) The group and the group analyst's pregnancies. Group Analysis 27: 51–61.

Roberts J, Pines M (1991) The Practice of Group Analysis. London: Tavistock/Routledge.

Rose C (2001) Working in supervision groups. Counselling and Psychotherapy Journal 12: 6–9.

Sharpe M (1995) The Third Eye: Supervision of Analytic Groups. London: Routledge.

Thomas P, Davison S, Rance C (2001) Clinical Counselling in Medical Settings. Hove: Brunner-Routledge.

Varma V (1997) Stress in Psychotherapists. London: Routledge.

Wertheimer A (2001) A Special Scar: The Experiences of People Bereaved by Suicide. Hove: Brunner-Routledge.

Which? (2003) A guide to using the Small Claims Court. Which? February.

Wilke G, Freeman S (2001) How To Be a Good Enough GP: Surviving and Thriving in the New Primary Care Organisations. Abingdon: Radcliffe Medical Press.

Winnicott D (1975) Hate in the countertransference. In: Through Paediatrics to Psychoanalysis: Collected Papers. London: Karnac Books (Originally published in 1958 by Basic Books, New York; paper first published in 1947).

Winnicott D (1979) Hospital care supplementing intensive psychotherapy in adolescence. In: The Maturational Processes and the Facilitating Environment: Studies in the Theory of Emotional Development, pp. 242–8. London: Hogarth Press/Institute of Psycho-Analysis.

Index